Heart Jewel

This book is published under the auspices of the
NKT-IKBU International Temples Project
and the profit from its sale is designated for public
benefit through this fund.
[Reg. Charity number 1015054 (England)]
Find out more:
tharpa.com/benefit-all-world-peace

VENERABLE GESHE KELSANG
GYATSO RINPOCHE

Heart Jewel

THE ESSENTIAL PRACTICES OF
KADAMPA BUDDHISM

THARPA PUBLICATIONS
UK • US • CANADA
AUSTRALIA • ASIA

First published 1991
Second edition 1997
Reprinted 2002, 2006, 2009, 2015

Tharpa Publications UK
Conishead Priory
Ulverston, Cumbria
LA12 9QQ, UK

Tharpa Publications US
47 Sweeney Road
Glen Spey, NY 12737
USA

There are Tharpa Publications offices around the world,
and Tharpa books are published in most major languages.
See page 222 for contact details.

© New Kadampa Tradition – International Kadampa
Buddhist Union 1991, 1997

Cover painting of Je Tsongkhapa and his two Sons
descending from Tushita Pure Land.

Library of Congress Control Number: 2002104950

British Library Cataloguing in Publication Data
A catalogue record for this book is
available from the British Library.

ISBN 978-0-948006-56-2 – paperback
ISBN 978-1-910368-37-4 – ePub
ISBN 978-1-910368-38-1 – kindle

Set in Palatino by Tharpa Publications
Printed and bound in the United Kingdom by Bell and Bain Ltd.

Paper supplied from well-managed forests and other controlled
sources, and certified in accordance with the rules of the
Forest Stewardship Council.

Contents

Illustrations

Acknowledgements

In the autumn of 1990, the students of Manjushri Kadampa Meditation Centre had the great good fortune to receive from the precious and fully realized Master, Venerable Geshe Kelsang Gyatso Rinpoche, a complete series of clear and inspiring teachings on the Guru yoga of Je Tsongkhapa according to the Segyu lineage. These teachings have now been published as the present book.

In this book, Venerable Geshe Kelsang establishes the authenticity and unique qualities of Je Tsongkhapa and the New Kadampa Tradition, thereby helping to promote this pure tradition throughout the world for succeeding generations. We thank the author most deeply for this inestimable kindness.

We would also like to thank all the students of the author who, with great skill and dedication, edited the book and prepared it for publication.

Roy Tyson,
Administrative Director,
Manjushri Kadampa Meditation Centre,
April 1997.

Preface

This book presents two practices revealed by Manjushri, the Wisdom Buddha. The first is a special Guru yoga in which we visualize our Spiritual Guide as Je Tsongkhapa, who himself is an emanation of Buddha Manjushri. By relying upon this practice we can purify negativity, accumulate merit and receive blessings. In this way, we will naturally accomplish all the realizations of the stages of the path of Sutra and Tantra, and in particular we will attain a very special Dharma wisdom.

The second practice is a method for relying upon the Dharma Protector. Through this practice we can overcome obstacles to our practice and create favourable conditions so that we can nurture and increase our pure Dharma realizations.

These two practices are the essential practices of the New Kadampa Tradition of Mahayana Buddhism. They are both included in the sadhana *Heart Jewel*, which can be found in Appendix III. By practising this sadhana regularly and sincerely, we will make our precious human life extremely meaningful and we will definitely reap a harvest of pure Dharma realizations. Eventually we will come to experience the supreme joy of full enlightenment.

PART ONE

The Guru Yoga of
Je Tsongkhapa

Je Tsongkhapa and his two Sons descending from Tushita Pure Land

Introduction

The commentary to the sadhana *Heart Jewel* is given under three main headings:

1 The instruction of the Guru yoga of Je Tsongkhapa according to the Segyu lineage
2 Relying upon the Dharma Protector
3 Dedication

The instruction of the Guru yoga of Je Tsongkhapa according to the Segyu lineage is presented in two parts:

1 Introduction
2 The actual practice of the instruction

The introduction has three parts:

1 Je Tsongkhapa
2 The history and lineage of the instruction
3 The benefits of this practice

JE TSONGKHAPA

In *Root Tantra of Manjushri* Buddha Shakyamuni made a prediction about how Manjushri would later emanate as Je Tsongkhapa:

After I pass away
And my pure doctrine is absent,
You will appear as an ordinary being,
Performing the deeds of a Buddha
And establishing the Joyful Land, the great Protector,
In the Land of the Snows.

This verse reveals the special qualities of Je Tsongkhapa. The third line explains that although he was an enlightened being, a manifestation of the Wisdom Buddha Manjushri, Je Tsongkhapa did not reveal himself to be a special being but always appeared in the aspect of an ordinary practitioner. In particular he never made a public display of his miracle powers or clairvoyance, and he encouraged his disciples to follow his example by not revealing any special powers they might have attained.

Instead of revealing miracle powers, Je Tsongkhapa mainly worked to establish pure Buddhadharma throughout Tibet. By giving teachings and showing a good example, he led many beings to gain pure, authentic realizations of Sutra and Tantra. This is the meaning of the fourth line of the verse.

The phrase 'Joyful Land' in the fifth line is the name of Buddha Maitreya's Pure Land, known as 'Tushita' in Sanskrit or 'Ganden' in Tibetan, which is where Je Tsongkhapa went after he passed away. During his life Je Tsongkhapa established a great monastery in Tibet called 'Ganden Monastery', and he spread throughout Tibet a pure doctrine that became known as the 'Ganden doctrine'. This doctrine is a special, pure Buddhadharma that comes from Manjushri's wisdom. It is called 'the great Protector' because it protects all living beings from the ocean of samsaric suffering. All of this indicates that Je Tsongkhapa is a manifestation of Buddha Maitreya, who is the Protector of the hundreds of Deities of the Joyful Land. These days, the tradition of Je Tsongkhapa is known as the 'Gelug', or 'Virtuous Tradition', and his followers are known as 'Gelugpas'; but the original name of 'Ganden' came from Buddha Shakyamuni. This is the meaning of the fifth line.

As Buddha had predicted, Je Tsongkhapa appeared in Tibet, the Land of the Snows, where he lived from 1357 to 1419. When he was born, a drop of his mother's blood fell to the ground, and later a white sandal tree with a hundred thousand leaves grew at that spot. On each of the leaves, there appeared an image of Buddha Sengei Ngaro, who is the same mental continuum as Buddha Manjushri. This indicates that the child was a manifestation of Manjushri. Later, the third Dalai Lama, Sonam Gyatso, said that this precious tree was an object of offerings and respect, and he moved it to a nearby monastery where he placed it inside a silver stupa with many precious jewels and made extensive offerings to it. This monastery became known as 'Kumbum Monastery', or 'The Monastery of a Hundred Thousand Images'. Eventually other similar trees grew around the stupa and their leaves also bore special images. On some there appeared the letters of Manjushri's mantra, OM AH RA PA TSA NA DHI, and on others the seed-letter of Manjushri, the letter DHI. These leaves were regarded as very precious, and when they fell in the autumn people would gather them and grind them into powder. Through tasting this powder many people have been able to cure diseases and increase their wisdom.

Je Tsongkhapa showed a perfect example of how to build the foundation for the spiritual path, how to progress on that path, and how to complete it. First he studied the entire Dharma of Sutra and Tantra by relying sincerely upon his Spiritual Guides, and then he put all this knowledge into practice and demonstrated the attainment of all the realizations from relying upon the Spiritual Guide up to the Union of No More Learning, or Buddhahood. Since then, thousands of practitioners have attained the ultimate happiness of Buddhahood within one life by following Je Tsongkhapa's example and sincerely practising his teachings. Even today, faithful practitioners who follow Je Tsongkhapa's pure Dharma can accomplish these results.

If, instead of giving teachings and setting a pure example, Je Tsongkhapa had mainly demonstrated his own good qualities by displaying miracle powers and other forms of clairvoyance, we would have received no benefit from his actions. What we need is not displays of miracle powers but a clear example of how to enter an unmistaken spiritual path, how to practise that path comfortably and smoothly, and how to complete it successfully. This is the actual method for solving our daily problems. Since Je Tsongkhapa provided us with just such an example, we should recognize his immense kindness and develop unchanging faith and respect for him.

Je Gendundrub, the first Dalai Lama, wrote a special praise to Je Tsongkhapa called *Song of the Eastern Snow Mountain*, or *Shargangrima* in Tibetan. In this song, he says to Je Tsongkhapa:

For the fortunate people of Tibet, the Land of the
    Snows, your kindness, O Protector, is inconceivable.
Especially for myself, Gendundrub,
The fact that my mind is directed towards Dharma
Is due solely to your kindness, O Venerable Father
    and Sons.

From now until I attain enlightenment
I shall seek no refuge other than you.
O Venerable Father and Sons
Please care for me with your compassion.

Although I cannot repay your kindness, O Protector,
I pray that, with my mind free from the influence of
    attachment and hatred,
I may strive to maintain your doctrine and cause it
    to flourish
Without ever giving up this endeavour.

Just visualizing Je Tsongkhapa with faith is a powerful method for receiving the blessings of all the Buddhas, and, if we have strong faith, simply keeping a statue of Je Tsongkhapa in our house will cause that place to become a holy environment and will protect us from poverty.

When Je Tsongkhapa passed away, the whole country was overwhelmed with sorrow at the loss of their precious Teacher. Not only could they no longer see him directly but, since there were very few representations of him, most people were unable to see even his likeness. Consequently, many craftsmen set about making statues and painting tangkhas of him. Although Je Tsongkhapa had not publicly displayed his miracle powers while he was alive, after he passed away he performed many miracles through these statues and tangkhas. Eight statues in particular have since become very famous. They are known as:

(1) Je she par ma (The Venerable One who Disappeared with a Smile)

(2) Je nga dra ma (The Venerable One who is a Better Likeness)

(3) Je shen pen ma (The Venerable One who is More Beneficial to Others)

(4) Je ku thim ma (The Venerable One who Dissolved into the Body)

(5) Je nam pur ma (The Venerable One who Rose into Space)

(6) Je tsong pon gelek ma (The Venerable Chief Merchant Gelek)

(7) Je tso dog ma (The Venerable One who Pacifies Conflicts)

(8) Je ling pur ma (The Venerable One Gone to Another Land)

The story of the first statue is as follows. At one time, a humble practitioner tried to find a statue of Je Tsongkhapa for his retreat but was unsuccessful, so during his retreat he made a small statue and placed it on his shrine. For him, this statue was like the living Je Tsongkhapa, and every day before beginning his meditation he made offerings and prostrations in front of it. One day as he rose from meditation he noticed that the statue was gradually melting into light. As he watched, the statue suddenly smiled and, rising into space, completely disappeared. The meditator was astonished and could hardly believe what he had seen. After reflecting for a long time, he decided to go to his Teacher to tell him what had happened. His Teacher was delighted and told him to make another statue exactly like the previous one. This he did, and it is this statue that subsequently became known as, 'The Venerable One who Disappeared with a Smile'.

The second and third statues were made by two craftsmen who were engaged in a friendly contest to see who was the more skilled at making statues. They took the two statues to a high Lama to adjudicate. As the Lama was examining them with a faithful mind, one statue spoke, saying 'I am a better likeness.' Then the other statue retorted, 'But I am more beneficial to others.' This is how these two famous statues received their names.

The fourth statue is named after one that belonged to a practitioner called Nyungne Lama, whose main practice was the Guru yoga of Je Tsongkhapa. He used to keep a statue of Je Tsongkhapa on his shrine, and he regarded this statue as the living Je Tsongkhapa. Each day, he would practise Guru yoga from going for refuge up to dissolving Guru Tsongkhapa into his heart. Because he practised so sincerely, he developed a very pure heart and attained a special experience of concentration. One day, while visualizing Je Tsongkhapa dissolving into his heart, he experienced his statue actually dissolving into him; and when he rose from meditation the statue on his shrine had completely disappeared. After this, he quickly attained many high realizations. News of this event spread, and the craftsman who had made the statue became very famous. Later he made another statue of Je Tsongkhapa, to which he gave the name, 'The Venerable One who Dissolved into the Body'.

The fifth statue belonged to a monastery where it was often seen by one particularly sincere practitioner to rise into space and then return to its place on the shrine. Because of this, the statue became known as, 'The Venerable One who Rose into Space'.

The sixth statue was made by a government minister who was a faithful disciple of Je Tsongkhapa, and Je Tsongkhapa himself had blessed it. One day, however, an evil person out of jealousy stole the statue and, taking it a long way away, threw it into a large river. Some time later, an important merchant called Gelek was travelling on horseback in that area when he noticed a brightly coloured rainbow standing vertically in space, apparently emerging from the bed of a river. Thinking that this was an unusual sign, he decided to spend the night nearby. The next morning the rainbow was still there and so he decided to investigate further. Although the local people could see nothing in the river, Gelek was not convinced. Securing himself with ropes he waded into the icy river and dived to the bottom. There he found the statue of Je Tsongkhapa radiating brightly coloured rainbow lights. When he came to the surface, the onlookers were astonished to see that he had not drowned, and even more astonished to see the precious statue that he was holding. Since it was the chief merchant Gelek who retrieved the statue, it subsequently became known as, 'The Venerable Chief Merchant Gelek'.

The seventh statue comes from a part of eastern Tibet where at one time there was prolonged civil war. The local people longed for the fighting to stop, and so they went to a nearby Lama who was renowned as a great meditator and asked him what they should do. He told them to construct a large statue of Je Tsongkhapa in their town and make offerings and requests in front of it. This they did, and soon afterwards the fighting stopped and peace prevailed throughout the region. This statue later became known as, 'The Venerable One who Pacifies Conflicts'.

The eighth statue is named after a much revered statue of Je Tsongkhapa that mysteriously disappeared from Tibet. Pure practitioners with clairvoyance realized that the statue had gone to another land far away where the ground was strewn with diamonds and where the language and customs were completely different. They also realized that the statue was benefiting the people of that land, and so they decided to make another one similar to it and named it, 'The Venerable One Gone to Another Land'.

Miracles such as these are not confined to ancient times. Even today there are many statues and other representations of Je Tsongkhapa that possess special qualities. For example, there was one Geshe called Geshe Jatse whom I knew well when I was at Sera Monastery in Tibet. When he had completed his Geshe training, he withdrew to a mountain cave to do retreat, and remained

Je Sherab Senge

there, living just like Milarepa, for the rest of his life. When he died, his many disciples, together with a large number of onlookers, went to the cave to pay their respects, and to their astonishment saw that Geshe Jatse's statue of Je Tsongkhapa had grown teeth and hair. I heard this account directly from these disciples, some of whom I knew well.

My first Teacher in philosophy at Ngamring Jampaling Monastery was called Geshe Palden. At one time he did a long close retreat on Je Tsongkhapa counting *Migtsema* prayers. At the end of his retreat, an image of Je Tsongkhapa appeared on one of the beads of his mala. He showed this to me and I saw it very clearly.

There are many other stories such as these which show that, even in these impure times, faithful practitioners can receive unceasing blessings from Je Tsongkhapa.

THE HISTORY AND LINEAGE OF THE INSTRUCTION

The Guru yoga of Je Tsongkhapa according to the Segyu lineage was originally taught by Buddha Manjushri as part of a special scripture known as the *Kadam Emanation Scripture*. It was extracted from this scripture by Je Tsongkhapa himself. These days, the practice is known as *Ganden Lhagyema* in Tibetan, or *The Hundreds of Deities of the Joyful Land* in English. The name derives from the fact that in the first verse we invite Je Tsongkhapa to descend from the heart of Buddha Maitreya, who is known as the 'Protector of the hundreds of Deities of the Joyful Land'.

Je Tsongkhapa passed this instruction to Je Sherab Senge, who was one of his main disciples. Je Sherab Senge was born in the upper part of Tibet called Tsang. He was a very holy meditation master and scholar who had thousands of disciples, including Je Gendundrub, the first Dalai Lama. He was the holder of the lineage of the Tantric teachings of Je Tsongkhapa and, as predicted by Je Tsongkhapa, he established Gyume Tantric College in central Tibet and Segyu Tantric College in the upper part of Tibet.

Je Sherab Senge passed this instruction to Dulnagpa Palden Sangpo, who was one of his main disciples. Palden Sangpo was also born in Tsang, in a town called Tanagdo near Tashilhunpo Monastery, and he was ordained at Narthang Monastery. After receiving this instruction, he practised it sincerely and as a result gained very high spiritual realizations. He was able to help many sick people by curing serious diseases and by pacifying obstacles through healing actions performed in conjunction with the *Migtsema* prayer.

In general, there are many people who are harmed by spirits called 'Behar'. These spirits enter into people's bodies, causing them to become insane, interfering with their spiritual development, or causing untimely death. Once, while Palden Sangpo was engaged in a retreat on the *Migtsema* prayer at a place called Sepu, a Behar spirit began to harm a rich family who lived nearby. Many of their relatives had already been killed by such spirits, and now this spirit was trying to enter into the body of the son of the family. The members of the family were very worried and they requested Palden Sangpo to stop the spirit harming their son. Palden Sangpo accepted their request and gave the father a number of beads from the mala he had used during his *Migtsema* recitation. He told him, 'When the spirit enters your son's body, immediately place one bead at every exit to your house. This may cause the spirit to cry out in terror, and if this happens, call me.' The father did exactly as Palden Sangpo had said, and in this way trapped the spirit in his house. The spirit was terrified and cried, 'I want to escape from this house but many powerful and terrifying wrathful beings are preventing me.'

The father immediately went to Palden Sangpo and requested him to come to his house. When Palden Sangpo arrived he asked the spirit, 'How can you inflict harm on many mother sentient beings when you yourself cannot bear even this slight suffering? From now on, you must not harm anyone else. If you do not promise to stop harming others, Yamantaka will not let you go.' The spirit replied, 'I follow the orders of the chief Behar spirit. If I do not harm anyone, my powers will diminish and I will suffer. Please do not ask so much of me, please reduce the commitment.' Palden Sangpo told the spirit, 'At least you must promise me that you will not harm anyone who recites the *Ganden Lhagyema* or *Migtsema* prayers', and the spirit said, 'Yes, I can promise you this.' Palden Sangpo then gathered up the beads of his mala from the exits to the house and the spirit immediately left the boy's body and fled. The boy became normal again and did not suffer further. Later, people clearly realized that anyone who recites the *Ganden Lhagyema* and *Migtsema* prayers will be protected from harm by Behar spirits.

Both the *Ganden Lhagyema* and the *Migtsema* prayers come from the *Kadam Emanation Scripture*. This scripture, which is the same nature as Manjushri's wisdom, cannot be seen by ordinary beings, and the instructions it contains are not written in ordinary letters. So that ordinary beings could see these prayers, Palden Sangpo wrote them out in ordinary letters, in the form of prose. Later, Khedrub Sangye Gyatso wrote the verses that we now recite.

Je Palden Sangpo passed this instruction on to Gyuchen Gendunpai, who passed it on to Gyuchen Tashipa, who passed it on to Je Samdrub Gyatso, who passed it on to Tsondrupa, who passed it on to Dorje Sangpo, who passed it on to Khedrub Sangye Gyatso. Eventually the instruction reached Je Phabongkhapa and Vajradhara Trijang Rinpoche, spiritual Father and Son.

This lineage is an uncommon close lineage that comes from Buddha Shakyamuni to Manjushri, and directly from Manjushri to Je Tsongkhapa, Je Sherab Senge, and so on. Through the kindness of Je Sherab Senge, Je Palden Sangpo and Khedrub Sangye Gyatso, this instruction flourished throughout Tibet. Since these Lamas came from the area called Se, in the region of Tashilhunpo Monastery, the lineage is called the 'Segyu lineage'.

THE BENEFITS OF THIS PRACTICE

When we practise the Guru yoga of Je Tsongkhapa according to the Segyu lineage, we meditate on our root Guru in the aspect of Je Tsongkhapa – the embodiment of Avalokiteshvara, Manjushri and Vajrapani – offer the

seven limbs and the mandala offering, make requests
with the *Migtsema* prayer, and then engage in the stages of
the practice of profound meditations. Through practising
sincerely in this way, we can pacify all our negative karma
and obstacles and increase our merit, life span and Dharma
realizations. In particular, because Je Tsongkhapa is at once
an emanation of Avalokiteshvara (the embodiment of all
Buddhas' compassion), Manjushri (the embodiment of all
Buddhas' wisdom) and Vajrapani (the embodiment of all
Buddhas' power), we can easily increase our realizations
of compassion, wisdom and spiritual power. Of these, it
is especially important to increase our wisdom because
wisdom is the antidote to ignorance, the root of all our
suffering. As Buddha says in the *Perfection of Wisdom
Sutra*, those who lack wisdom are like blind people who
continually experience problems and suffering because
they cannot see. The best method for increasing our
wisdom, and thereby protecting ourself from suffering, is
to practise the Guru yoga of Je Tsongkhapa, because Je
Tsongkhapa is a manifestation of the wisdom of all the
Buddhas.

On the basis of pacifying our negativity and obstacles
and increasing our life span, merit, compassion, wisdom
and spiritual power, if we rely upon this practice we will
easily gain all the realizations of Sutra and Tantra and
eventually attain the Union of No More Learning, or
Buddhahood. Because followers of Je Tsongkhapa have
a special connection with him, all these beneficial results
of entering into Je Tsongkhapa's doctrine can be achieved
with great ease by practising this Guru yoga.

As we have seen, Palden Sangpo controlled Behar spirits, protected many people from untimely death, and pacified their suffering through the practice of reciting the *Ganden Lhagyema* and *Migtsema* prayers. In the account mentioned above, the Behar spirit saw the beads of Palden Sangpo's mala as terrifying wrathful beings, who in reality were Yamantaka. This clearly indicates that accomplishing the attainment of Je Tsongkhapa has the same function as accomplishing the attainment of Yamantaka, reciting the *Migtsema* prayer has the same function as reciting the mantra of Yamantaka, meditating on Je Tsongkhapa has the same function as meditating on Yamantaka, and so on. 'Yamantaka', or 'Shin je she' in Tibetan, means 'opponent of outer, inner and secret obstacles'. Thus, the practices of *Ganden Lhagyema* and *Migtsema* are powerful methods for pacifying these three types of obstacle. Outer obstacles include harm from human beings or non-human beings, dangers from the outer elements such as fire and water, different kinds of accident, and lacking the necessary conditions for spiritual practice. Inner obstacles include sickness, strong delusions and negative thoughts that arise within our mind. Secret obstacles are ordinary appearances, ordinary conceptions and subtle dualistic appearance.

Although both Yamantaka and Je Tsongkhapa are manifestations of Manjushri, for followers of Je Tsongkhapa the practices of *Ganden Lhagyema* and *Migtsema* are more powerful than the practice of Yamantaka. There are three reasons for this: (1) followers of Je Tsongkhapa have a direct connection with Je Tsongkhapa's doctrine; (2) the practices of *Ganden Lhagyema* and *Migtsema* were taught directly by Manjushri himself, and Je Tsongkhapa is the principal Guru of this practice; and (3) the instruction of *Ganden Lhagyema* and *Migtsema* has the uncommon close lineage mentioned above. When we accomplish the practice of *Ganden Lhagyema* and *Migtsema*, we accomplish not only the practices of wrathful and peaceful Manjushri, but also the practices of Avalokiteshvara and Vajrapani.

Mahasiddha Menkhangpa said:

The unmistaken Dharma is Lamrim, Lojong and Mahamudra.

Here, 'Mahamudra' refers to Vajrayana Mahamudra, which contains the practices of both generation stage and completion stage of Secret Mantra. The instruction on these three Dharmas – Lamrim (the stages of the path), Lojong (training the mind) and Mahamudra – is the heart of Je Tsongkhapa's doctrine and the very essence of Buddhadharma. To gain the realizations of these three Dharmas, we must receive into our mind the powerful blessings of Je Tsongkhapa by sincerely engaging in the practice of the *Ganden Lhagyema* and *Migtsema* prayers.

Mahasiddha Menkhangpa and the Panchen Lama, Palden Yeshe, composed eleven different instructions on ritual healing practices in conjunction with the *Migtsema* prayer. These are practices: (1) to make rain for crops, (2) to gather clouds, (3) to cure the 'drib' disease, a physical disease caused by spirits that makes people fall and become unconscious without any visible reasons, (4) to avoid harm from weapons, (5) to prevent future drib diseases, (6) to cure wind, or 'lung', diseases, (7) to cure physical and mental disabilities, (8) to protect against thieves, robbers, and enemies, (9) to pacify obstacles to growing crops, such as insects, (10) to find food, and (11) to pacify obstacles when travelling. Those who have completed an action close retreat of *Migtsema* can perform these healing practices to benefit others.

Altogether there are one hundred and eight ritual practices in conjunction with the *Migtsema* prayer that have been written by different authors. They are all methods for helping sentient beings.

The practice of *Migtsema* is very important for fulfilling both one's own and others' wishes. Through not understanding the benefits of reciting the *Migtsema* prayer, many people disregard this practice. Others ignore it, thinking that it is just a small practice. Some even think, 'This practice is small, whereas I am a great practitioner.' Such an attitude is a wrong conception. Once a Mongolian minister asked the Panchen Lama, Palden Yeshe, to give him a small practice that he could do every day because he was otherwise very busy. The Panchen Lama asked him what kind of practice he wanted, and the Mongolian replied that he would like to receive the instruction on the *Migtsema* practice. The Panchen Lama was surprised and said, 'How can you say that the practice of *Migtsema* is a small practice? There is no greater practice than this; it contains the meaning of all Buddha's eighty-four thousand teachings!'

Accumulating Merit

THE ACTUAL PRACTICE OF THE INSTRUCTION

The actual practice of the instruction of the Guru yoga of Je Tsongkhapa according to the Segyu lineage has three parts:

1 The actual practice
2 An explanation of the *Migtsema* prayer
3 How to do a close retreat of *Migtsema*

The actual practice has two parts:

1 The practice during the meditation session
2 The practice during the meditation break

The practice during the meditation session has five parts:

1 The preliminary practices of going for refuge and generating bodhichitta
2 Inviting the Field for Accumulating Merit
3 Accumulating merit
4 Receiving attainments by making requests
5 Conclusion

THE PRELIMINARY PRACTICES OF GOING FOR REFUGE AND GENERATING BODHICHITTA

This has four parts:

1 The objects of refuge
2 Generating the causes of going for refuge
3 The prayer of going for refuge
4 Generating bodhichitta

THE OBJECTS OF REFUGE

We visualize the objects of refuge by contemplating as follows:

In the space before me is the living Buddha Shakyamuni surrounded by all the Buddhas and Bodhisattvas, like the full moon surrounded by stars.

GENERATING THE CAUSES OF GOING FOR REFUGE

We generate the causes of going for refuge by contemplating as follows:

I and all my kind mothers, fearing samsara's torments, turn to Buddha, Dharma, and Sangha, the only sources of refuge. From now until enlightenment, to the Three Jewels we go for refuge.

THE PRAYER OF GOING FOR REFUGE

Having generated the causes of refuge, we now go for refuge while reciting the following prayer three times:

I and all sentient beings, until we achieve enlightenment,
Go for refuge to Buddha, Dharma, and Sangha.

GENERATING BODHICHITTA

We then generate a motivation of bodhichitta while reciting the following prayer three times:

Through the virtues I collect by giving and other
perfections,
May I become a Buddha for the benefit of all.

INVITING THE FIELD FOR ACCUMULATING MERIT

The principal beings in the Field for Accumulating Merit in this practice are Je Tsongkhapa and his two main disciples, Gyaltsabje and Khedrubje. Je Tsongkhapa is a manifestation of Manjushri, the nature of all Buddhas' wisdom; Gyaltsabje a manifestation of Avalokiteshvara, the nature of all Buddhas' compassion; and Khedrubje a manifestation of Vajrapani, the nature of all Buddhas' power.

We invite Je Tsongkhapa and his two spiritual Sons to come from Joyful Land, Tushita, to the space before us. As mentioned before, Je Tsongkhapa went to Tushita after he passed away and so we begin by visualizing him together with his two Sons at the heart of Buddha Maitreya within this Pure Land. This reminds us that Je Tsongkhapa and Buddha Maitreya are the same mental continuum.

Many great Teachers went to Tushita Pure Land after they passed away. Atisha, for example, told his faithful disciples, 'In my next life I will go to Joyful Land. Those who have faith in me will meet me there.' Accordingly, after he passed away Atisha went to Tushita Pure Land, where he appeared as a principal disciple of Maitreya called 'Stainless Space' (Tib. Namkha Drime). He gave Dharma teachings to his disciples in Tushita and sent many emanations to this world. Some time later, Atisha's main disciple, Dromtonpa, established Reting Monastery, and during the puja for blessing the monastery, known in Tibetan as the 'rabne puja', he requested Stainless Space to bless the monastery. Stainless Space did so by throwing flowers from Tushita onto the roof of the monastery. Later many practitioners of the Old Kadampa tradition, including Dromtonpa himself, chose to be reborn in Tushita so as to be close to their Spiritual Guide.

Just like Atisha, Je Tsongkhapa also went to Tushita Pure Land, where he appeared as a main Bodhisattva disciple of Maitreya called 'Essence of Manjushri' (Tib. Jampel Nyingpo). He gave many teachings to his disciples in Tushita and sent countless emanations to this world. Just as many practitioners of the Old Kadampa tradition chose to be reborn in Tushita to be close to their Spiritual Guide, Atisha, so many practitioners of the New Kadampa tradition, including Khedrubje and Gyaltsabje, chose to be reborn in this Pure Land so as to be close to Je Tsongkhapa.

To gain a rough image of what Tushita Pure Land is like, we can contemplate the following description:

To the north of this continent, Jambudipa, is Mount Meru, which has four stepped levels. On top of Mount Meru is

Land of the Thirty-three Heavens, the second abode of the desire realm gods; in the space above this is Land Without Combat, the third abode of the desire realm gods; and in the space above this is Joyful Land, the fourth abode of the desire realm gods. Just above this god realm is the Pure Land of Buddha Maitreya, which is also known as Joyful Land, or Tushita.

Beings who abide in Tushita Pure Land do not experience ageing, sickness, or any other suffering, and they acquire whatever they need effortlessly. In this place, there is not even the sound of poverty or fighting, and no danger from fire, water, wind, or earth. The environment is completely pure, clean and very beautiful, and there are many objects of enjoyment such as precious mountains, wishfulfilling trees, beautiful lakes and pools. In the trees, many delightful birds, which are emanations of Maitreya, make sounds that reveal the meaning of Dharma. There are also many beautiful gardens filled with exquisite jewels, heavenly flowers, and precious bathing pools in which fortunate young gods and goddesses play. The whole ground is made of jewels and is completely pure and smooth. Just touching it gives rise to bliss. In the centre of this Pure Land is the Yiga Chodzin Palace, where Buddha Maitreya lives with a retinue of thousands of Bodhisattvas.

To invite Je Tsongkhapa Father and Sons to the space before us we begin by visualizing them at the heart of Buddha Maitreya, indicating that they will come from Maitreya's Truth Body, the space of the Dharmakaya:

In the Yiga Chodzin Palace, on a jewelled throne supported by eight snow lions, sits Buddha Maitreya, who has a golden-coloured body. His two hands at the level of his heart in the gesture of turning the Wheel of Dharma hold flowers from a naga tree. These support a wheel and a long-necked vase. He is seated on a throne with his feet on the ground, indicating his readiness to descend from Tushita to this world. At his heart is Je Tsongkhapa, with Gyaltsabje to his right and Khedrubje to his left. They sit on a cluster of clouds which resemble a mass of fresh, white curd, and which are a manifestation of Maitreya's compassion. They each wear the saffron robes of an ordained person.

Having visualized this clearly, we recite the verse from the sadhana inviting Je Tsongkhapa and his two Sons, together with all the Buddhas and Bodhisattvas, to come to the space in front of us as objects for accumulating merit. We strongly imagine that, due to our invitation prayer, Je Tsongkhapa Father and Sons come from the clouds of compassion at Maitreya's heart to the space before us:

White clouds billow from Maitreya's heart and descend to the space in front of us, just like a ball of wool unravelling with one end of the thread remaining connected to Maitreya's heart. At the same time, Je Tsongkhapa and his two Sons descend and sit on thrones on the clouds.

This way of inviting Je Tsongkhapa and his Sons is very special because it indicates that, from the space of Maitreya's Truth Body, clouds of his compassion for the beings of this world arise, and as a result a rain of Dharma teachings continually descends upon the beings of this world through Je Tsongkhapa and his emanations.

At this point we visualize as follows:

In the space in front of us, there are three jewelled thrones with the central throne slightly higher than the other two. Each throne is supported by eight snow lions. On the central throne, on a lotus, moon and sun cushion, sits our root Guru in the aspect of Je Tsongkhapa, who is the embodiment of Manjushri, Avalokiteshvara and Vajrapani. On the throne to his right, on a lotus, moon and sun cushion, sits Gyaltsabje, who is a manifestation of Avalokiteshvara. On the throne to his left, on a lotus, moon, and sun cushion, sits Khedrubje, who is a manifestation of Vajrapani.

Their bodies are made of wisdom light, and are white with a reddish tint. They wear the three robes of an ordained person, signifying that they have completed the perfection of the three moral disciplines; and yellow long-eared hats, signifying that they have completed the perfection of wisdom. They are sitting on jewelled thrones that are supported by eight lions, symbolizing their four fearlessnesses in general, and their four protections that protect sentient beings from the four maras in particular. The lotus, moon and sun cushions signify their complete purity of body and mind, their conventional bodhichitta, and their ultimate bodhichitta respectively. Their sitting in the vajra posture indicates that they have attained the Union of No More Learning.

Je Tsongkhapa's two hands at the level of his heart, in the gesture of turning the Wheel of Dharma, indicate that he can dispel the ignorance of sentient beings by giving teachings. He holds stems of upala flowers, which support a wisdom sword and a scripture of the Perfection of Wisdom Sutra in Eight Thousand Lines. *These signify that he principally teaches the profound Madhyamika-Prasangika view explained in the* Perfection of Wisdom Sutras *(symbolized by the scripture) by means of his omniscient wisdom (symbolized by the sword), motivated by love and compassion (symbolized by the two flowers). The right hands of the two Sons are at the level of their hearts in the gesture of expounding Dharma, and their left hands are in the gesture of meditative equipoise holding scriptures, signifying that Je Tsongkhapa's doctrine will spread throughout the world.*

At the centre of Je Tsongkhapa's crown chakra, on a lotus and moon cushion, is Manjushri, with an orange-coloured body, one face and two arms. At the centre of his throat chakra, on a lotus and moon cushion, is Avalokiteshvara, with a white-coloured body, one face and four arms. At the centre of his heart chakra, on a lotus and sun cushion, is Vajrapani, with a blue-coloured body, one face and two arms. They are all complete with their usual features, such as ornaments, clothes, gestures and implements. Je Tsongkhapa and his two Sons are surrounded by all the Buddhas and Bodhisattvas.

Visualizing in this way, we should strongly believe that Je Tsongkhapa and all the other holy beings are actually present in the space before us, and generate a mind of deep faith.

Since Maitreya is an enlightened being, he is the Protector of all sentient beings, but in the sadhana it says that Maitreya is the 'Protector of the hundreds of Deities of the Joyful Land'. This indicates that the hundreds of millions of fortunate beings who abide in Tushita Pure Land have a special opportunity to receive teachings directly from Maitreya. The words 'King of the Dharma' signify that Je Tsongkhapa is like the crown ornament of all the Dharma Teachers in Tibet, and that his Dharma teachings are the king of all teachings.

ACCUMULATING MERIT

We now offer the practice of the seven limbs to Je Tsongkhapa and all the other holy beings so as to accumulate a vast collection of merit that will enable us to fulfil all our spiritual hopes and wishes. For auspiciousness we begin with the limb of requesting the Spiritual Guide to remain for a long time, which is normally recited as the fifth limb.

BESEECHING THE SPIRITUAL GUIDE TO REMAIN FOR A LONG TIME

If the Spiritual Guides who lead sentient beings on spiritual paths were no longer to appear in this world, the people of this world would have no opportunity to go

Palden Sangpo

for refuge or to accumulate merit, and there would be no possibility of their escaping from the sufferings of samsara and gaining pure happiness. From a spiritual point of view, the world would be plunged into darkness. So as to prevent this happening, we now request the holy beings, the Buddhas, to remain for countless aeons as emanations who will lead sentient beings on the spiritual path. This practice is a very powerful method for accumulating merit, and is extremely important for the future happiness of sentient beings.

We strongly believe that Je Tsongkhapa in the space before us is in essence our Spiritual Guide and we imagine that he is smiling at us with delight, just like a mother delighted with her dearest child. We visualize Je Tsongkhapa surrounded by all the Gurus, Yidams, Buddhas and Bodhisattvas, and, by reciting the prayer from the sadhana, request them from the depths of our heart to remain with samsaric beings until samsara has ceased. We request them to remain as our supreme Field for Accumulating Merit so that we may sow the seeds of faith, cultivate the crops of the collections of merit and wisdom, and enjoy the ultimate harvest of full enlightenment.

PROSTRATION

Prostrations are a powerful method for purifying negative karma, sickness and obstacles, and for increasing our merit, our happiness and our Dharma realizations. Temporarily prostrations improve our physical health, and ultimately they cause us to attain a Buddha's Form Body. Generating faith in the holy beings is mental prostration, reciting praises to them is verbal prostration, and showing respect to them with our body is physical prostration. We can make physical prostrations by respectfully prostrating our entire body on the ground; by respectfully touching our knees, palms, and forehead to the ground; or by respectfully placing our palms together at the level of our heart.

To make special prostrations to Je Tsongkhapa we begin by contemplating the pre-eminent qualities of his mind, his speech and his body. Since Je Tsongkhapa has abandoned the obstructions to omniscience, his mind knows all phenomena without exception, and he realizes all conventional truths and all ultimate truths clearly, directly, and simultaneously. Simply hearing Je Tsongkhapa's speech causes fortunate beings to experience pure happiness, so for them his speech is a supreme ear ornament that gives rise to uncontaminated bliss. Je Tsongkhapa's body is extremely pleasing to behold because it is adorned with all the major signs and minor indications of a Buddha's Form Body. Thus, just by seeing Je Tsongkhapa's actual body or image, hearing his actual speech or his teachings, or remembering his good qualities, we accumulate a vast collection of merit and wisdom. Remembering this, we generate deep faith in Je Tsongkhapa and then, in order to make powerful prostrations to him, we imagine that from every pore of our body we emanate another body, and from every pore of these bodies we emanate yet more bodies, until our emanated bodies fill the entire world. Then, while reciting the verse from the sadhana, we strongly believe that all these countless bodies make prostrations to Je Tsongkhapa, the principal Field for Accumulating Merit, and to all the other Gurus, Yidams, Buddhas, Bodhisattvas, Dakas, Dakinis and Dharma Protectors.

OFFERING

We imagine that all the oceans, lakes, pools, springs and rivers in the world transform into nectar for drinking, pure bathing water, and perfume. We think that these pure waters, together with all the flowers, incense, light, food and music in the world, have the nature of exalted wisdom and function to cause the holy beings to experience uncontaminated bliss. Then we offer all these substances, each in their own aspect such as nectar for drinking, bathing water and so forth, to the holy Gurus – Je Tsongkhapa and his retinue – while reciting the verse from the sadhana.

PURIFICATION

Since beginningless time we have created many negativities through our bodily, verbal and mental actions. If these actions ripen on us they will result in our taking countless rebirths as hell beings, hungry spirits and animals. Moreover, many times in our previous lives we broke our spiritual commitments and the three sets of vows – the Pratimoksha vows, the Bodhisattva vows and the Tantric vows. The result of these transgressions will be that our spiritual progress will be retarded and we will find it more difficult to gain realizations. Realizing this, we generate deep regret and decide very strongly not to repeat such actions in the future. With this thought, we purify our negativities by confessing them to the holy beings with the verse from the sadhana.

REJOICING

In his autobiography Je Tsongkhapa says that first he studied Dharma extensively, then he realized that all of Buddha's teachings are personal advice, and finally he gained deep realizations of Dharma through practising day and night. He then dedicated all his activities to the flourishing of pure Buddhadharma. In short, in this degenerate age Je Tsongkhapa showed the best example for Dharma practitioners to follow. He taught what pure Buddhadharma is, how to study and practise Dharma, and how to accomplish complete realizations. Contemplating this, we rejoice from the depths of our heart in his great deeds while reciting the verse from the sadhana.

REQUESTING THE TURNING OF
THE WHEEL OF DHARMA

Buddha Shakyamuni demonstrated the manner of attaining the great liberation of full enlightenment at Bodh Gaya, but if he had not subsequently taught the Dharma that he experienced, the people of this world would have had no chance to attain liberation from the ocean of samsaric suffering. Therefore, while Buddha was in meditative equipoise the gods Brahma and Indra made the following request to him:

Without a Protector to provide protection
The blind migrators of this world will fall into the
    lower realms;
O Treasure of Compassion, please rise from your
    meditation
And turn the Wheel of Dharma.

As a result of Brahma and Indra making this request, Buddha gave many Dharma teachings that are the medicine for curing the diseases of delusions. From that time until now, countless beings have attained complete liberation from samsaric suffering through sincerely practising Buddha's teachings. In a similar way, although there are many emanations of Je Tsongkhapa in the world, if they do not teach Je Tsongkhapa's Dharma the people of this world will have no chance to hear this special Dharma, put it into practice, and gain pure realizations. Therefore, by reciting the verse from the sadhana we make a special request for the turning of the Wheel of Dharma.

DEDICATION

There is a prayer that says:

By my riding the horse of virtue,
Directing it along correct paths with the reins of
    dedication,
And urging it with the whip of joyous effort,
May all beings reach the city of great liberation.

Since the attainment of great liberation depends upon pure Buddhadharma flourishing, we dedicate all our virtues to this end and pray that all sentient beings will thereby attain great enlightenment. We recite the verse from the sadhana.

OFFERING THE MANDALA

The word 'mandala' in this context means 'universe'. When we offer a mandala to the holy beings, we are offering everything – the whole universe with all its objects and all the beings who inhabit it. Since the merit we create when we make an offering accords with the nature of the offering, we mentally transform the whole universe into a Pure Land and imagine that all its objects are precious substances. We then imagine that we are offering this pure universe in our hands.

A child once filled a bowl with dust and, imagining that the dust was gold, offered it to Buddha Kashyapa. As a result of this pure offering, the child was reborn as the wealthy King Ashoka. Likewise, if we offer the world as a Pure Land filled with exquisite objects and precious symbols, we will experience special, pure results. If we wish to experience happiness in the future, and especially if we wish for spiritual attainments, we should offer a mandala every day.

For more information on the practice of the seven limbs and the mandala offering, see the book *Joyful Path of Good Fortune.*

Receiving Attainments

Receiving attainments by making requests has two parts:

1 Making requests
2 Receiving attainments

MAKING REQUESTS

In this context, there are three ways of making requests:

1 Making requests with regard to Je Tsongkhapa's outer qualities
2 Making requests with regard to Je Tsongkhapa's inner qualities
3 Making requests with regard to Je Tsongkhapa's secret qualities

MAKING REQUESTS WITH REGARD TO JE TSONGKHAPA'S OUTER QUALITIES

With regard to the qualities of scriptural knowledge and the skilful means to teach others, Avalokiteshvara, Manjushri and Vajrapani are unequalled among all the Bodhisattvas. In a similar way, with regard to these same qualities, Je Tsongkhapa, or Losang Dragpa, is unequalled among all the scholars of Tibet. Knowing this, with deep faith we make requests by reciting the following *Migtsema* prayer:

Tsongkhapa, crown ornament of the scholars of the Land of the Snows,
You are Avalokiteshvara, the treasury of unobservable compassion,
Manjushri, the supreme stainless wisdom,
And Vajrapani, the destroyer of the hosts of maras;
O Losang Dragpa I request you, please grant your blessings.
You have knowledge of all the scriptures;
Please bless me to become just like you.

MAKING REQUESTS WITH REGARD TO
JE TSONGKHAPA'S INNER QUALITIES

With regard to their inner realizations, Avalokiteshvara, Manjushri and Vajrapani are unequalled among all the Bodhisattvas; and, in a similar way, since he too possesses all these realizations, Je Tsongkhapa is unequalled among all the scholars of Tibet. Knowing this, with deep faith we make requests by reciting the following *Migtsema* prayer:

Tsongkhapa, crown ornament of the scholars of the Land of the Snows,
You are Avalokiteshvara, the treasury of unobservable compassion,
Manjushri, the supreme stainless wisdom,
And Vajrapani, the destroyer of the hosts of maras;

*O Losang Dragpa I request you, please grant your
    blessings.*
You have accomplished all the realizations;
Please bless me to become just like you.

MAKING REQUESTS WITH REGARD TO
JE TSONGKHAPA'S SECRET QUALITIES

Manjushri is the essence of the wisdom of all the Buddhas,
Avalokiteshvara is the essence of the compassion of all the
Buddhas, Vajrapani is the essence of the spiritual power
of all the Buddhas; and Je Tsongkhapa is the synthesis of
these three holy beings. Knowing this, with deep faith we
make requests by reciting the following *Migtsema* prayer:

*Tsongkhapa, crown ornament of the scholars of the Land
    of the Snows,*
*You are Avalokiteshvara, the treasury of unobservable
    compassion,*
Manjushri, the supreme stainless wisdom,
And Vajrapani, the destroyer of the hosts of maras;
*O Losang Dragpa I request you, please grant your
    blessings.*
You are the synthesis of all these holy beings;
Please bless me to become just like you.

When we are emphasizing the study of Dharma scriptures
we recite principally the first version of the *Migtsema* prayer;
when we are emphasizing gaining realizations by engaging
in actual practices we recite principally the second version;
and when we are emphasizing the practice of Secret Mantra
we recite principally the third version.

RECEIVING ATTAINMENTS

This has two parts:

1 Purifying impurities
2 Accomplishing wisdom and attaining the realizations of the stages of the path

PURIFYING IMPURITIES

While reciting the *Migtsema* prayer and concentrating on its meaning, we sincerely request Je Tsongkhapa and his two Sons to dispel the inner darkness of our ignorance and other delusions and to purify all our negative karma and obstacles. Then we imagine that, from the hearts of the Venerable Father and Sons, there radiate white rays of light, which are hollow like straws. At our crown, the tips of all three rays of light merge together to become one. We then strongly imagine that, from the hearts of Je Tsongkhapa and his two Sons, white wisdom-nectar, in the aspect of milk, flows through the rays of light and enters our body through our crown. Our body fills with light and wisdom-nectar, which purifies our ignorance and all our other delusions, as well as all our negative karma and obstacles. Our entire body becomes the nature of wisdom light. We meditate on this feeling single-pointedly for as long as possible.

ACCOMPLISHING WISDOM AND ATTAINING THE REALIZATIONS OF THE STAGES OF THE PATH

This has two parts:

1 Accomplishing wisdom
2 Attaining the realizations of the stages of the path

ACCOMPLISHING WISDOM

This has two parts:

1 An introduction to the seven types of wisdom
2 The actual practice

AN INTRODUCTION TO THE SEVEN TYPES OF WISDOM

We can accomplish seven types of wisdom:

1 Great wisdom
2 Clear wisdom
3 Quick wisdom
4 Profound wisdom
5 The wisdom of expounding Dharma
6 The wisdom of spiritual debate
7 The wisdom of composing Dharma books

GREAT WISDOM

If we can understand easily, perfectly, and without difficulty all the objects that we need to abandon, such as true sufferings and true origins, and all the objects that we need to accomplish, such as true cessations and true paths, this indicates that we have great wisdom.

CLEAR WISDOM

If we can clearly distinguish the subtle characteristics of phenomena, such as the sixteen characteristics of the four noble truths, this indicates that we have clear wisdom.

QUICK WISDOM

Whenever doubts, wrong conceptions, or unknowing manifest in our mind, if we can dispel them quickly by gaining a perfect understanding of the actual nature of these objects, this indicates that we have quick wisdom.

PROFOUND WISDOM

If we can perfectly understand all the profound meanings of the scriptures without any difficulty, this indicates that we have profound wisdom.

THE WISDOM OF EXPOUNDING DHARMA

When we are giving Dharma teachings we need a special wisdom that realizes how much the listeners can understand and which subjects are suitable for them. Moreover, we need to understand the correct order of the subjects we are going to talk about – what to say first, what to say next, and so on. We need to understand perfectly the meaning of all that we are going to talk about, and we need to understand special methods, such as suitable analogies and conclusive reasons, that will clarify the meaning for others. In addition we must also understand what qualities we need to become a perfect Teacher, and how to teach the Dharma as explained in Lamrim teachings. The wisdom understanding all of this is the wisdom of expounding Dharma.

THE WISDOM OF SPIRITUAL DEBATE

Since there are so many different views in the world, both religious and non-religious, which are contrary to the views that are presented in the Dharma teachings, we need a special wisdom that understands the methods for dispelling such views through skilful spiritual debate or discussion. In this way we can lead many people to correct spiritual paths, just as Dharmakirti was able to lead many people to correct views by engaging in actions such as spiritual debate.

THE WISDOM OF COMPOSING DHARMA BOOKS

Dharma books are the eyes through which sentient beings can see the spiritual paths to liberation and enlightenment, the light by which they can dispel the darkness of ignorance, and the Spiritual Guide from whom they can receive reliable advice. Therefore, composing authentic Dharma books brings immense benefit to many living beings and causes Buddhadharma to remain for a long time in this world. However, to compose authentic Dharma books we need a special wisdom. We need perfect understanding of the subject matter and the confidence to write about it, and we also need the wisdoms arisen from listening, contemplating, and meditating. With these we can develop the special wisdom that has the complete ability to compose Dharma books.

Je Sangye Gyatso

THE ACTUAL PRACTICE

The actual practice of receiving attainments has seven parts: receiving the attainment of great wisdom, and so on.

RECEIVING THE ATTAINMENT OF GREAT WISDOM

First, by reciting the *Migtsema* prayer we make strong requests to the Venerable Father and Sons so that we may be able to attain the realization of great wisdom. We then imagine white rays of light, which are hollow like straws, coming from the hearts of Je Tsongkhapa and his two Sons, and merging into one at the point where the tips touch the crown of our head. We imagine that the great wisdom of the Venerable Father and Sons, in the aspect of orange-coloured nectar, flows from their hearts through the rays of light and enters our body through our crown. Our body is completely filled with nectar, all the atoms of which are in the aspect of tiny Manjushris. From all these tiny bodies of Manjushri, which are the commitment beings, infinite rays of light radiate throughout the ten directions and draw back the great wisdom of all the Buddhas in the aspect of Manjushri's Form Body. These wisdom beings dissolve into the tiny commitment beings within our body and become inseparably one with them. All these countless tiny Manjushris then dissolve into our root mind at our heart. Our root mind and the tiny Manjushris mix completely, like water mixing with water, and we strongly imagine that we have received the great wisdom of all the Buddhas. We meditate single-pointedly on this feeling for a while.

RECEIVING THE ATTAINMENT OF CLEAR WISDOM

We begin by requesting the attainment of clear wisdom by reciting the *Migtsema* prayer. The basic visualization is the same as above, except that this time we visualize the clear wisdom of Je Tsongkhapa and his Sons flowing from their hearts in the form of orange-coloured nectar, all the atoms of which are in the aspect of the tiny letters of Manjushri's mantra: OM AH RA PA TSA NA DHI. The nectar completely fills our body, and all the tiny letters emanate infinite rays of light throughout the ten directions, drawing back the clear wisdom of all the Buddhas in the same aspect. The wisdom beings dissolve into the commitment beings as before, and then all the countless tiny OM AH RA PA TSA NA DHI letters dissolve into our root mind at our heart and mix inseparably with it. We strongly imagine that we have received the clear wisdom of all the Buddhas, and meditate single-pointedly on this feeling for a while.

RECEIVING THE ATTAINMENT OF QUICK WISDOM

We begin by requesting the attainment of quick wisdom by reciting the *Migtsema* prayer. Then we visualize the quick wisdom of Je Tsongkhapa and his Sons flowing from their hearts in the form of orange-coloured nectar, all the atoms of which are in the aspect of tiny DHI seed-letters. The nectar completely fills our body, and all the tiny DHI letters emanate infinite rays of light throughout the ten directions, drawing back the quick wisdom of all the Buddhas in the same aspect. The wisdom beings dissolve into the commitment beings as before, and then all the countless tiny DHI letters dissolve into our root mind at our heart and mix inseparably with it. We strongly imagine that we have received the quick wisdom of all the Buddhas, and meditate single-pointedly on this feeling for a while.

RECEIVING THE ATTAINMENT OF PROFOUND WISDOM

We begin by requesting the attainment of profound wisdom by reciting the *Migtsema* prayer. Then we visualize the profound wisdom of Je Tsongkhapa and his Sons flowing from their hearts in the form of orange-coloured nectar, all the atoms of which are in the aspect of tiny Dharma scriptures and Manjushri's wisdom sword. The nectar completely fills our body, and all the tiny scriptures and swords emanate infinite rays of light throughout the ten directions, drawing back the profound wisdom of all the Buddhas in the same aspect. The wisdom beings dissolve into the commitment beings as before, and then all the countless tiny scriptures and swords dissolve into our root mind at our heart and mix inseparably with it. We strongly imagine that we have received the profound wisdom of all the Buddhas, and meditate single-pointedly on this feeling for a while.

RECEIVING THE ATTAINMENT OF THE WISDOM OF EXPOUNDING DHARMA

We begin by requesting the attainment of the wisdom of expounding Dharma by reciting the *Migtsema* prayer. Then we visualize the wisdom of expounding Dharma of Je Tsongkhapa and his Sons flowing from their hearts in the form of orange-coloured nectar, all the atoms of which are in the aspect of Dharma books that we are going to explain. The nectar completely fills our body, and all the tiny books emanate infinite rays of light throughout the ten directions, drawing back the wisdom of expounding Dharma of all the Buddhas in the same aspect. The wisdom beings dissolve into the commitment beings as before, and then all the countless tiny books dissolve into our root mind at our heart and mix inseparably with it. We strongly imagine that we have received the wisdom of expounding Dharma of all the Buddhas, and meditate single-pointedly on this feeling for a while.

RECEIVING THE ATTAINMENT OF THE WISDOM OF SPIRITUAL DEBATE

We begin by requesting the attainment of the wisdom of spiritual debate by reciting the *Migtsema* prayer. Then we visualize the wisdom of spiritual debate of Je Tsongkhapa and his Sons flowing from their hearts in the form of orange-coloured nectar, all the atoms of which are in the aspect of tiny wheels of swords. The nectar completely fills our body, and all the tiny wheels of swords emanate infinite rays of light throughout the ten directions, drawing back the wisdom of spiritual debate of all the Buddhas in the same aspect. The wisdom beings dissolve into the commitment beings as before, and then all the countless tiny wheels of swords dissolve into our root mind at our heart and mix inseparably with it. We strongly imagine that we have received the wisdom of spiritual debate of all the Buddhas, and meditate single-pointedly on this feeling for a while.

RECEIVING THE ATTAINMENT OF THE WISDOM OF COMPOSING DHARMA BOOKS

We begin by requesting the attainment of the wisdom of composing Dharma books by reciting the *Migtsema* prayer. Then we visualize the wisdom of composing Dharma books of Je Tsongkhapa and his Sons flowing from their hearts in the form of orange-coloured nectar, all the atoms of which are in the aspect of tiny Dharma books on the subject upon which we are going to write and tiny wheels of swords. The nectar completely fills our body, and all the tiny books and wheels of swords emanate infinite rays of light throughout the ten directions, drawing back the wisdom of composing Dharma books of all the Buddhas in the same aspect. The wisdom beings dissolve into the commitment beings as before, and then all the countless tiny books and wheels of swords dissolve into our root mind at our heart and mix inseparably with it. We strongly imagine that we have received the wisdom of composing Dharma books of all the Buddhas, and meditate single-pointedly on this feeling for a while.

ATTAINING THE REALIZATIONS OF THE STAGES OF THE PATH

Now, by reciting the *Migtsema* prayer, we make strong requests so that we may be able to attain all the realizations of the stages of the path. Then, while concentrating without distraction on the meaning of what we are saying, we recite the *Prayer of the Stages of the Path* composed by Je Tsongkhapa, known in Tibetan as *Yonten Zhirgyurma*:

Je Phabongkhapa

The path begins with strong reliance
On my kind Teacher, source of all good;
O Bless me with this understanding
To follow him with great devotion.

This human life with all its freedoms,
Extremely rare, with so much meaning;
O Bless me with this understanding
All day and night to seize its essence.

My body, like a water bubble,
Decays and dies so very quickly;
After death come results of karma,
Just like the shadow of a body.

With this firm knowledge and remembrance
Bless me to be extremely cautious,
Always avoiding harmful actions
And gathering abundant virtue.

Samsara's pleasures are deceptive,
Give no contentment, only torment;
So please bless me to strive sincerely
To gain the bliss of perfect freedom.

O Bless me so that from this pure thought
Come mindfulness and greatest caution,
To keep as my essential practice
The doctrine's root, the Pratimoksha.

Just like myself all my kind mothers
Are drowning in samsara's ocean;
O So that I may soon release them,
Bless me to train in bodhichitta.

But I cannot become a Buddha
By this alone without three ethics;
So bless me with the strength to practise
The Bodhisattva's ordination.

By pacifying my distractions
And analyzing perfect meanings,
Bless me to quickly gain the union
Of special insight and quiescence.

When I become a pure container
Through common paths, bless me to enter
The essence practice of good fortune,
The supreme vehicle, Vajrayana.

The two attainments both depend on
My sacred vows and my commitments;
Bless me to understand this clearly
And keep them at the cost of my life.

By constant practice in four sessions,
The way explained by holy Teachers,
O Bless me to gain both the stages,
Which are the essence of the Tantras.

May those who guide me on the good path,
And my companions all have long lives;
Bless me to pacify completely
All obstacles, outer and inner.

May I always find perfect Teachers,
And take delight in holy Dharma,
Accomplish all grounds and paths swiftly,
And gain the state of Vajradhara.

After this, we recite the prayer for receiving blessings and purifying:

From the hearts of all the holy beings, streams of light
and nectar flow down, granting blessings and purifying.

If we combine our Lamrim meditations with this practice, we will gradually accomplish all the realizations of the stages of the path.

CONCLUSION

We begin the concluding stages by imagining that our mind is in the aspect of an orange-coloured letter DHI, which is standing on an eight-petalled lotus and moon cushion inside the central channel at the centre of our heart. We then make the following request:

O Glorious and precious root Guru,
Please sit on the lotus and moon seat at my heart.
Please care for me with your great kindness,
And grant me the blessings of your body, speech, and mind.

We imagine that all the other Buddhas and Bodhisattvas dissolve into Gyaltsabje and Khedrubje, and that the two Sons then dissolve into Je Tsongkhapa. With delight Guru Tsongkhapa comes to our crown, where he diminishes to the size of a thumb. We then make another request:

O Glorious and precious root Guru,
Please sit on the lotus and moon seat at my heart.
Please care for me with your great kindness,
And bestow the common and supreme attainments.

After making this request, we imagine that Guru Tsongkhapa enters our body and, descending through the central channel, reaches the centre of our throat chakra. We then make another request with the following prayer:

O Glorious and precious root Guru,
Please sit on the lotus and moon seat at my heart.
Please care for me with your great kindness,
And remain firm until I attain the essence of enlightenment.

We now imagine that Guru Tsongkhapa descends to the centre of our heart chakra and dissolves into our mind, which is in the aspect of the letter DHI. Throughout this visualization it is important not to forget the thread of clouds that connects Je Tsongkhapa to Buddha Maitreya in Tushita Pure Land. We recognize that Guru Tsongkhapa at our heart is the synthesis of our mind, Je Tsongkhapa, and our root Guru; and we meditate on this recognition for a while. At this point, if we wish, we can meditate on the Mahamudra that is the union of bliss and emptiness, which is the very essence of Vajrayana practice.

Finally the eight petals of the lotus, which are the nature of light, close to form the shape of a heart, leaving no gaps between the petals. The heart-shaped lotus is then entirely encircled by the letters: OM AH RA PA TSA NA DHI SU MA TI KIR TI SHI RI BHA DRA AH THI TA NA AH THI TI TE KUR BEN TU, which cover it completely without leaving any gaps. We contemplate that the heart-shaped lotus is now inside the protection circle of the mantra and, if we wish, recite the mantra a few times. Then we finish the session by reciting dedication prayers and auspicious prayers.

THE PRACTICE DURING THE MEDITATION BREAK

During the meditation break we should always remain mindful of Guru Tsongkhapa, who is inseparable from our root mind at our heart. Whenever we eat or drink, we should imagine that we are making offerings to Guru Tsongkhapa at our heart; if people make offerings, prostrations, or other gestures of respect to us, we should immediately offer these mentally to Guru Tsongkhapa at our heart; whenever we practise any kind of healing or blessing action for the benefit of others, we should think that the power of this action comes principally from Guru Tsongkhapa at our heart; and whenever we are in danger or frightened, we should immediately remember Guru Tsongkhapa at our heart and recall that he is the nature of Vajrapani. In addition we should continually try to improve our faith in Je Tsongkhapa by contemplating his teachings and his many other pre-eminent qualities.

If we wish to be reborn in Tushita Pure Land easily, it is essential always to remember the thread of clouds that directly connects Guru Tsongkhapa at our heart with Buddha Maitreya's heart because this indicates that we have a special connection with Buddha Maitreya. Even if we experience sudden death, providing we remember this thread of clouds we will definitely be reborn in Tushita Pure Land because our consciousness will follow the pathway of this thread directly to Maitreya's heart. This is an actual transference of consciousness. Thus, if we sincerely practise *Ganden Lhagyema* and *Migtsema* each day, and remember the thread of clouds at the time of death, we will definitely be reborn in Tushita Pure Land.

Vajradhara Trijang Rinpoche

The Migtsema *Prayer*

AN EXPLANATION OF THE *MIGTSEMA* PRAYER

The *Migtsema* prayer is as follows:

> Tsongkhapa, crown ornament of the scholars of the
> Land of the Snows,
> You are Avalokiteshvara, the treasury of
> unobservable compassion,
> Manjushri, the supreme stainless wisdom,
> And Vajrapani, the destroyer of the hosts of maras;
> O Losang Dragpa I request you, please grant your
> blessings.

As mentioned before, this prayer was composed by
Manjushri and revealed in the *Kadam Emanation Scripture*.
Je Tsongkhapa extracted it and, changing the first and the
fifth lines, offered it as a praise to his Guru, Je Rendapa.
Rendapa, however, returned it in its original form to Je
Tsongkhapa, saying, 'This is more suitable for you.'

The explanation of the *Migtsema* prayer has two parts:

1 An explanation of the first line
2 An explanation of the remaining four lines

AN EXPLANATION OF THE FIRST LINE

Just as crown ornaments are unequalled among ornaments, so Je Tsongkhapa is unequalled among all Tibetan scholars. There are three ways in which we can understand this:

1 With regard to the pre-eminent qualities of his teachings, Je Tsongkhapa is unequalled among all Tibetan scholars

2 With regard to his practical example, Je Tsongkhapa is unequalled among all Tibetan scholars

3 With regard to his Dharma activities, Je Tsongkhapa is unequalled among all Tibetan scholars

WITH REGARD TO THE PRE-EMINENT QUALITIES OF HIS TEACHINGS, JE TSONGKHAPA IS UNEQUALLED AMONG ALL TIBETAN SCHOLARS

It is only through Je Tsongkhapa's teachings that we can understand the four pre-eminent attributes of the stages of the path: (1) that none of Buddha's teachings are contradictory; (2) that we can take all Buddha's teachings as personal advice and put them into practice; (3) that we can easily realize Buddha's ultimate intention; and (4) that we can naturally become free from the great fault and from all other faults. Although the root text of the stages of the path, Atisha's *Lamp for the Path to Enlightenment* (Tib. *Lam dron*), possesses these four pre-eminent attributes, we cannot discover this simply by reading this text because it is only a few pages long. Thus we need also to study the clear and extensive explanations given in Je Tsongkhapa's Lamrim teachings.

Within Je Tsongkhapa's teachings, we find special presentations of how to develop the realization of renunciation, which is the main path to liberation; how to develop bodhichitta, which is the main path to enlightenment; and how to develop the correct view of emptiness, which is the method for eradicating ignorance. These special explanations cannot be found in other teachings.

Without relying upon Je Tsongkhapa's teachings, it is difficult during these degenerate times to reach an unmistaken understanding of the precise nature of tranquil abiding (Tib. zhi ne) and actual superior seeing (Tib. lhag tong), or to know how to begin these practices, how to sustain them, and how to complete them. Moreover, without relying upon Je Tsongkhapa's teachings we will also find it difficult to understand precisely the nature of samsara and actual liberation.

Furthermore, it is only in Je Tsongkhapa's teachings that we find the uncommon, clear, and profound instructions on how the realizations of the four classes of Secret Mantra develop. This is particularly true of the development of the stages of Highest Yoga Tantra: clear light, illusory body, the union that needs learning, and the Union of No More Learning. We can find clear explanations of these profound subjects only in Je Tsongkhapa's teachings.

These pre-eminent qualities of Je Tsongkhapa's teachings are not possessed even by the kings of the Tantras,

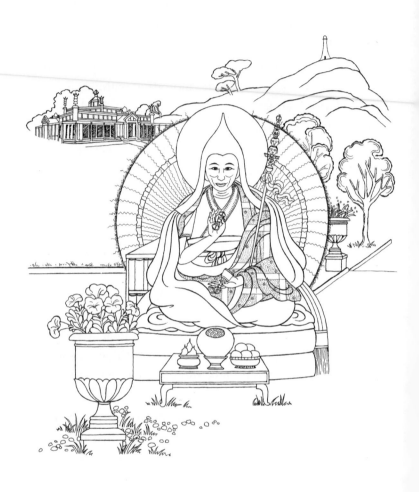

Dorjechang Kelsang Gyatso Rinpoche

Guhyasamaja Tantra and *Heruka Tantra*, which were composed by Vajradhara, nor by the king of the Sutras, the *Perfection of Wisdom Sutra*.

There are many commentaries to the stages of the path, training the mind, Mahamudra, Tantric practices, and philosophical subjects written by followers of Je Tsongkhapa. These include the books *Joyful Path of Good Fortune*, *Universal Compassion*, *Mahamudra Tantra*, *Great Treasury of Merit*, *Clear Light of Bliss*, *The New Guide to Dakini Land*, *Modern Buddhism*, *The Oral Instructions of Mahamudra* and *Ocean of Nectar*. All of these books are based on Je Tsongkhapa's teachings.

In summary, because Je Tsongkhapa's teachings have no equal in Tibet, Je Tsongkhapa himself is unequalled among all Tibetan scholars. Because a crown ornament is unequalled among ornaments, Manjushri refers to Je Tsongkhapa as the 'crown ornament of the scholars of the Land of the Snows'.

WITH REGARD TO HIS PRACTICAL EXAMPLE, JE TSONGKHAPA IS UNEQUALLED AMONG ALL TIBETAN SCHOLARS

There are three different aspects to Je Tsongkhapa's spiritual practice: outer, inner, and secret. With regard to the first, Je Tsongkhapa engaged in all the practices of moral discipline that Buddha taught in the *Vinaya Sutras*, such as the two hundred and fifty-three disciplines of a fully ordained monk. From this point of view he was like a pure Hinayana practitioner who was completely free from the downfalls of the Pratimoksha vows. Because of this, all his bodily actions were immaculately pure and beautiful, and people naturally appreciated him and developed faith in him.

With regard to the second aspect, Je Tsongkhapa engaged in all the practices of moral discipline that Buddha taught in the Mahayana Sutras, and was completely free from the downfalls of the Bodhisattva vows, such as the eighteen root downfalls and forty-six secondary downfalls. All his actions of body, speech, and mind were motivated solely by bodhichitta, and all his daily actions accorded with the Bodhisattva's way of life.

With regard to the third aspect, Je Tsongkhapa engaged in all the practices of moral discipline taught by Buddha in his Vajrayana teachings. As a result of his pure practice of Deity yoga and the yoga of the union of great bliss and emptiness, he was completely free from gross and subtle ordinary appearances and conceptions. From Je Tsongkhapa's way of practising the Vajrayana, his disciples can clearly understand how to lay the foundation for Vajrayana practice, how to progress in this practice, and how to complete it. They can also realize that the practices of the Hinayana, Mahayana and Vajrayana taught by Buddha in the scriptures are not contradictory but can all be put into practice by a single practitioner.

In summary, from among all the scholars in Tibet, Je Tsongkhapa showed the best example for practising the Hinayana, Mahayana and Vajrayana.

WITH REGARD TO HIS DHARMA ACTIVITIES, JE TSONGKHAPA IS UNEQUALLED AMONG ALL TIBETAN SCHOLARS

As mentioned above, in *Root Tantra of Manjushri* Buddha predicted that Je Tsongkhapa would perform the deeds of a Buddha. As Buddha predicted, Je Tsongkhapa dedicated all his activities to spreading throughout the world the special Buddhadharma that comes from Manjushri's wisdom. To this end he was tireless in giving teachings on the extensive and profound Dharma, and in writing special Dharma books. So lucid and authentic were his books that even scholars of other traditions praised them. For example, Tagtsang Lotsawa praised Je Tsongkhapa's works as a great treasury of excellent explanation that had never been seen before. Je Tsongkhapa wrote sixteen volumes that clearly reveal the entire Buddhadharma by means of a very special presentation. His writings have exactly the same pre-eminent qualities as his teachings. The main reason why Je Tsongkhapa's books and teachings have such special qualities is that he is a manifestation of the wisdom of all the Buddhas.

To help his special Dharma flourish, Je Tsongkhapa established many great monasteries, gathered thousands of disciples who gained advanced realizations, and organized special spiritual programmes in his monasteries. In this way, the whole of Tibet was filled with fortunate practitioners who had met Je Tsongkhapa's doctrine.

Avalokiteshvara

AN EXPLANATION OF THE REMAINING FOUR LINES

The compassion of all the Buddhas appears in the form of Avalokiteshvara, the wisdom of all the Buddhas appears as Manjushri, and the spiritual power of all the Buddhas appears as Vajrapani. Since Je Tsongkhapa is the synthesis of these three holy beings, if with deep faith we sincerely make requests to him by reciting the *Migtsema* prayer, we will gain a realization of great compassion like that of Avalokiteshvara, supreme stainless wisdom like that of Manjushri, and great power in destroying obstacles like that of Vajrapani. Gaining these realizations is extremely important for everyone because temporarily they will help us to solve all our daily problems and ultimately they will enable us to attain complete liberation from suffering, and full enlightenment. Realizing this, we should strive tirelessly to make requests to Je Losang Dragpa by reciting the *Migtsema* prayer.

The last four lines can also be understood as follows. The words 'treasury of unobservable compassion' reveal the stages of the vast path, the words 'supreme stainless wisdom' reveal the stages of the profound path, and the words 'destroyer of the hosts of maras' reveal the stages of the Vajrayana path. With respect to the Buddha families, Avalokiteshvara belongs to the Pema family, the family of Buddha Amitabha; Manjushri belongs to the Tathagata family, the family of Buddha Vairochana; and Vajrapani belongs to the Vajra family, the family of Buddha Akshobya. From this point of view, therefore, Avalokiteshvara is the vajra speech of the Buddhas,

Manjushri is the vajra body of the Buddhas, and Vajrapani is the vajra mind of the Buddhas. Thus, these four lines indicate that if we sincerely make requests with strong faith to Je Losang Dragpa by reciting the *Migtsema* prayer, we can easily gain realizations of the stages of the vast path, the profound path and the Vajrayana path; and through this we can attain the vajra body, speech and mind of a Buddha. Understanding this, we should strive continuously to practise the *Migtsema* prayer.

We can also apply the explanation of the three ways of making requests mentioned above to these different meanings of the *Migtsema* prayer.

Close Retreat

How to do a close retreat of *Migtsema* has four parts:

1 What is a retreat?
2 The necessary conditions for a close retreat of *Migtsema*
3 The preparations for a close retreat of *Migtsema*
4 The practice of an action close retreat of *Migtsema*

WHAT IS A RETREAT?

On retreat we stop all forms of business and extraneous activities so as to emphasize a particular spiritual practice. There are three kinds of retreat: physical, verbal and mental. We engage in physical retreat when, with a spiritual motivation, we isolate ourself from other people, activities and noise, and disengage from extraneous and meaningless actions. We engage in verbal retreat when, with a spiritual motivation, we refrain from meaningless talk and periodically keep silence. We engage in mental retreat by preventing distractions and strong delusions such as attachment, anger, jealousy and strong self-grasping from arising, and by maintaining mindfulness and conscientiousness.

Manjushri

If we remain in physical and verbal retreat but fail to observe mental retreat, our retreat will have little power. Such a retreat may be relaxing, but, if we do not prevent strong delusions from arising, our mind will not be at peace, even on retreat. However, keeping physical and verbal retreat will help us to keep mental retreat, and for this reason Shantideva, in *Guide to the Bodhisattva's Way of Life*, praises the first two kinds of retreat.

A close retreat is a retreat in which we practise special methods that cause us to draw closer to the attainments of a Tantric Deity. We engage in a close retreat of signs when we remain in retreat until a correct sign of attainment manifests. We engage in a close retreat of time when we do a retreat for a definite period of time, such as six months; or, alternatively, when we do either a long or short close retreat every year at the same time.

There are two kinds of close retreat of numbers: a close retreat of actions and a great close retreat. There are also longer and shorter close retreats of actions. On a long close retreat of actions of *Migtsema*, we recite the *Migtsema* prayer four hundred thousand times, and on a short close retreat of actions of *Migtsema*, we recite the *Migtsema* prayer one hundred thousand times.

THE NECESSARY CONDITIONS FOR A
CLOSE RETREAT OF *MIGTSEMA*

For success in this practice, we need to gain at least some experience of the stages of the path so that we have a special motivation of bodhichitta and some understanding of emptiness. We also need strong faith in Je Tsongkhapa and his doctrine, and our daily practice must belong to the pure lineage of Je Tsongkhapa. Upon this basis, we need to have received the blessing empowerment of Je Tsongkhapa. We also need to understand clearly how to practise this instruction through having listened to or read authentic commentaries.

THE PREPARATIONS FOR A CLOSE RETREAT OF *MIGTSEMA*

We prepare a suitable meditation room, thinking:

In each session during this retreat, I will invite Guru Tsongkhapa and all the holy beings to this place; therefore I need to clean my room and prepare special offerings.

With this motivation we first clean our room and the area around it. In front of statues or pictures of Buddha Shakyamuni, Je Tsongkhapa and our root Guru, we set out torma offerings and other offerings. We should set up three tormas, for which we can use cakes, honey, biscuits or chocolates. Since these tormas must remain for the duration of the retreat, we should not use substances that perish quickly. In front of the torma offerings we set out two or more rows of offering bowls for the in-front-generated Deities. These should be arranged starting from the right hand of the Deity (our left hand) in the following sequence: nectar for drinking, water for the feet, flowers, incense, light, perfume and food. Then in front of these we set out another row of offering bowls for ourself, the self-generated Deity, starting from our right hand. Other pure offerings can also be set out anywhere on the shrine.

In front of our meditation cushion, on a small table, we arrange our vajra, bell and mala. On the first day of the retreat, before the first actual session, we perform the extensive, the middling, or the condensed Dharma Protector sadhana to prevent obstacles to our retreat. The middling and condensed Dharma Protector sadhanas can be found in Appendix III. Then on the evening of the first day we start the first session of the retreat.

THE PRACTICE OF AN ACTION CLOSE RETREAT OF *MIGTSEMA*

This has two parts:

1 The practice during the meditation session
2 The practice during the meditation break

THE PRACTICE DURING THE MEDITATION SESSION

This has three parts:

1 Preliminary practices
2 The actual practice
3 Conclusion

Vajrapani

PRELIMINARY PRACTICES

We engage in the practice of *The Hundreds of Deities of the Joyful Land* (*Ganden Lhagyema*) from going for refuge and generating bodhichitta up to and including dissolving Guru Tsongkhapa into our mind at our heart, by reciting the sadhana *King of the Dharma*, which can be found in Appendix III.

THE ACTUAL PRACTICE

This has six parts:

1 Purifying our body and mind by meditating on emptiness
2 Transforming the basis of imputation for our I by generating ourself as Guru Tsongkhapa
3 Meditating on divine pride
4 Meditating on clear appearance
5 Reciting the mantras
6 The practice of the in-front-generation

PURIFYING OUR BODY AND MIND BY MEDITATING ON EMPTINESS

Having dissolved Guru Tsongkhapa into our mind at our heart, our mind becomes the nature of great bliss. With this feeling of great bliss, we imagine that from the heart of Je Tsongkhapa, who is inseparable from our mind, infinite rays of light radiate, pervading all worlds and their inhabitants. These melt into light and dissolve into our body. Our body then melts into light and dissolves into Je Tsongkhapa, who is one nature with our mind. Our mind, Je Tsongkhapa, then becomes smaller and smaller and finally dissolves into emptiness. We perceive nothing but emptiness, and we meditate on this emptiness single-pointedly for as long as possible.

TRANSFORMING THE BASIS OF IMPUTATION FOR OUR I BY GENERATING OURSELF AS GURU TSONGKHAPA

We contemplate as follows:

From this state of emptiness, there appears a jewelled throne supported by eight great lions. Upon this, from a letter PAM, there appears an eight-petalled lotus, and upon this, from a letter AH, there appears a moon mandala. In the centre of the moon, my mind appears in the aspect of an orange-coloured letter DHI. This then transforms into a sword, which is marked by a letter DHI. From this, light rays radiate, making offerings to all the Superior beings and fulfilling the welfare of all living beings. All the rays of light gather back into the sword, which completely transforms, and I arise as the great Je Tsongkhapa, the King of the Dharma of the three realms and the essence of all the Conquerors. I have a completely pure body, speech and mind.

My body, which is made of wisdom light, is white with a reddish tint. I have one face and two arms, and wear the three saffron-coloured robes of an ordained person and a golden long-eared Pandit's hat. My two hands are at the level of my heart in the gesture of turning the Wheel of Dharma. They hold between the thumbs and forefingers the stems of upala flowers, which blossom at the level of my right and left ears. On the flower to my right is a wisdom sword, and on the flower to my left is a scripture of the Perfection of Wisdom Sutra in Eight Thousand Lines.

My body is adorned with all the signs and indications of a Buddha, and is clear and translucent, the nature of light. I sit with my legs crossed in the vajra posture in the midst of a mass of brilliant light that radiates from my body.

At the centre of my crown chakra, on a lotus and moon cushion, is Manjushri, who has an orange-coloured body with one face and two arms; at the centre of my throat chakra, on a lotus and moon cushion, is Avalokiteshvara, who has a white-coloured body with one face and four arms; and at the centre of my heart chakra, on a lotus and sun cushion, is Vajrapani, who has a blue-coloured body with one face and two arms. They are complete with all their usual features, such as ornaments, clothes, gestures, and implements.

At Manjushri's heart is a white letter OM, at Avalokite- shvara's heart is a red letter AH, and at Vajrapani's heart is a blue letter HUM.

We visualize rays of light radiating from the HUM and inviting Guru Tsongkhapa surrounded by all the Buddhas to come from Tushita Pure Land, and we imagine that

Je Tsongkhapa

they all come to the space in front of us and dissolve into Guru Tsongkhapa. When we say 'DZA' we imagine Guru Tsongkhapa comes to our crown, when we say 'HUM' we imagine that he dissolves into us, when we say 'BAM' we imagine that Guru Tsongkhapa mixes with us, and when we say 'HO' we imagine that we become inseparably one. Now we strongly believe that our body is the body of the Wisdom Buddha in the aspect of Je Tsongkhapa and that our mind is the mind of the Wisdom Buddha. Focusing on our body and mind, the body and mind of Je Tsongkhapa, we develop divine pride, thinking, 'I am Je Tsongkhapa, the Wisdom Buddha.' At this stage we are no longer using our ordinary body and mind as the basis of imputation for our I, but are using only the body and mind of Je Tsongkhapa. This is the way of transforming the basis of imputation for our I. At this point we need to understand four things:

1 What is the basis of imputation for our I?
2 Why we need to change the basis of imputation for our I
3 How it is possible to change the basis of imputation for our I
4 How to change the basis of imputation for our I

WHAT IS THE BASIS OF IMPUTATION FOR OUR I?

What is a person's I or self? The I cannot be the body and mind because the I is the possessor, and the body and mind are the phenomena that are possessed. For example, when we say 'My body' or 'My mind', this indicates that we regard ourself as the possessor of our body and mind. However, although the I is not the body and mind, when the thought 'I' arises naturally in our mind, it does so only on the basis of perceiving our body or our mind. Thus, our body and mind are the basis for imputing our I.

WHY WE NEED TO CHANGE THE BASIS OF IMPUTATION FOR OUR I

When the thought 'I' arises within our mind, we automatically develop self-grasping that grasps at the I as existing from its own side. This thought is ignorance. It is the main cause of all the problems we experience and the root of samsara. Because our body and mind, which are the basis of imputation for our I, are contaminated aggregates, whenever we develop the thought 'I' we naturally develop the ignorance of self-grasping at the same time. For as long as we continue to use our present body and mind as the basis for imputing our I, we will never eradicate our ignorance of self-grasping, and so we will continually have to experience suffering. For this reason, we need to change the basis of imputation for our I.

HOW IT IS POSSIBLE TO CHANGE THE BASIS OF IMPUTATION FOR OUR I

In our previous lives we took countless bodies, and each time the basis of imputation for our I changed. When we were born human, the basis of imputation for our I was the body and mind of a human being, and when we were born as an animal, the basis of imputation for our I was the body and mind of an animal. Even within one life, the basis of imputation for our I changes many times. For instance, when we were a baby, the basis of imputation for our I was a baby's body and mind; when we were a child, the basis of imputation for our I was a child's body and mind; and when we grow old, the basis of imputation for our I will be the body and mind of an old person.

We may feel that even though we have had all these changes of body, there is no problem with regarding them all as our body because they are all of the same continuum; however it is not so easy to understand how another's body, which does not belong to us, can become the basis of imputation for our I. To understand this, we can consider the following. When we were conceived in the womb inside the union of our mother's ovum and father's sperm, our body, which at that time was like yoghurt mixed with red liquid, belonged to others. To begin with we had no idea of its being our body, but later, as we became more familiar with its continuum, we came to regard it as our own body and in this way it became the basis of imputation for our I. This clearly indicates that, with familiarity, another's body can become the basis of imputation for our I. In other words, 'my body' and 'other's body' are like 'this mountain' and 'that mountain'; they change depending upon our relative position.

In conclusion, having purified our ordinary body and mind by meditating on emptiness as explained above, we generate ourself as the Wisdom Buddha, Je Tsongkhapa. Then, using Je Tsongkhapa's body generated through our correct imagination as the basis of imputation for our I, we strongly develop divine pride, thinking, 'I am Je Tsongkhapa, the Wisdom Buddha.'

HOW TO CHANGE THE BASIS OF IMPUTATION FOR OUR I

We change the basis of imputation for our I by purifying the ordinary appearance of our body and mind through meditating on emptiness and then generating ourself as Je Tsongkhapa as explained above. Then we continually familiarize ourself with the meditations on divine pride and clear appearance. Eventually what was simply imagination becomes an actuality and we experience the pure body and mind of Je Tsongkhapa. This is the special way of changing the basis of imputation for our I through practising the spiritual path. Unlike the normal changes in the basis of imputation for our I, which occur from one life to the next due to karma, and which are the very process of samsara, this special method is the means for attaining release from samsara.

MEDITATING ON DIVINE PRIDE

After generating ourself as Je Tsongkhapa in this way, we make offerings and praises to ourself, the self-generated Deity, by reciting from the sadhana. We then engage in meditation on divine pride, contemplating as follows:

Because my ordinary body and mind have been purified,
I am no longer an ordinary being but Je Tsongkhapa, the

*Wisdom Buddha. I generated myself as Je Tsongkhapa
and invited Je Tsongkhapa to come from Tushita Pure
Land to dissolve into me and become inseparably one.
Therefore, I am Guru Tsongkhapa, the embodiment of all
the Buddhas.*

Having strongly generated this special feeling, we
meditate single-pointedly on it for as long as possible. We
need to train in this meditation until we develop strong
familiarity with it.

MEDITATING ON CLEAR APPEARANCE

With the divine pride established by the previous
meditation we then check precisely our environment and
body in order to perceive them clearly in our mind. We
try strongly to perceive our environment as Tushita Pure
Land, our house as Yiga Chodzin Palace, and our body as
Je Tsongkhapa's body, the body of the Wisdom Buddha.
We contemplate:

*I am sitting on a lotus, moon and sun cushion on a
jewelled throne supported by eight lions. The eight lions
are manifestations of my four fearlessnesses in general,
and of my four protections that protect sentient beings
from the four maras in particular. The lotus symbolizes
my complete purity of body, speech and mind; the moon
is a manifestation of my conventional bodhichitta; and
the sun is a manifestation of my ultimate bodhichitta.
My body is a manifestation of the wisdom of all the
Buddhas. My three robes are a manifestation of my*

realization of the perfection of the three moral disciplines, the long-eared hat is a manifestation of my ultimate view, the two flowers that I hold are manifestations of my realizations of love and compassion, the scripture is a manifestation of my speech, and the sword is a manifestation of my wisdom. My sitting in the full vajra posture symbolizes that I have accomplished the Union of No More Learning.

Through this contemplation, we try to perceive a general image of the whole environment, the palace, and the body of ourself, the self-generated Deity, in the aspect of Je Tsongkhapa's body. When we perceive this image, we meditate on it single-pointedly.

We train continually in this meditation until we perceive everything, from the environment to ourself as Je Tsongkhapa, clearly in our mind. This is the way to accomplish clear appearance. We can combine this meditation with the practice of training in tranquil abiding, which is explained in the books *Meaningful to Behold* and *Joyful Path of Good Fortune*.

RECITING THE MANTRAS

Having established divine pride, thinking 'I am Guru Tsongkhapa, the essence of all the Buddhas', and the clear appearance of our self-generated body as the Form Body of Guru Tsongkhapa, we then visualize that on a moon cushion at the heart of Manjushri abiding in the centre of our crown chakra, there is a letter DHI encircled clockwise by the orange-coloured letters OM AH RA PA TSA NA; on a moon cushion at the heart of Avalokiteshvara abiding in the centre of our throat chakra, there is a letter HRIH encircled clockwise by the white-coloured letters OM MANI PÄME HUM; and on a sun cushion at the heart of Vajrapani abiding in the centre of our heart chakra, there is a letter HUM encircled clockwise by the blue-coloured letters OM AH VAJRAPANI HUM HUM PHAT.

We then imagine that infinite rays of light radiate from the letter DHI and mantra at Manjushri's heart and touch the body and mind of all living beings. This light purifies the inner darkness of their ignorance, and they attain divine wisdom eyes that can see the reality of ultimate truth and all spiritual paths that lead to liberation. With this visualization we recite OM AH RA PA TSA NA DHI one hundred times. We then imagine that infinite rays of light radiate from the letter HRIH and mantra at Avalokiteshvara's heart and touch the body and mind of all living beings of the six realms. The light purifies all their negative karma and causes them to experience uncontaminated happiness. With this visualization we recite OM MANI PÄME HUM one hundred times. Then we imagine that infinite rays of light radiate from the letter HUM and mantra at Vajrapani's heart and touch the body and mind of all living beings. The light pacifies all their obstacles to gaining liberation and full enlightenment, and they all conquer the four maras and attain Buddhahood. With this visualization we recite OM AH VAJRAPANI HUM HUM PHAT one hundred times.

We now imagine that Manjushri dissolves into our body, whereby our body becomes the nature of Manjushri; Avalokiteshvara dissolves into our speech, whereby our speech becomes the nature of Avalokiteshvara; and Vajrapani dissolves into our mind, whereby our mind becomes the nature of Vajrapani.

Then on a moon cushion at our heart we visualize our mind in the aspect of an orange letter DHI encircled clockwise by the *Migtsema* prayer, or mantra. We imagine that infinite rays of light radiate from the letter DHI and *Migtsema* mantra to the ten directions and invite the blessings of the body, speech and mind of all the Buddhas in the aspect of white, red and blue rays of light. All these lights dissolve into our mind, the letter DHI at our heart, and we strongly believe that we have received the blessings of the body, speech, and mind of all the Buddhas.

With this visualization we recite the *Migtsema* mantra as many times as we can in each session. For a long action close retreat of *Migtsema*, we need to collect at least four hundred thousand *Migtsema* prayers, and for a short action close retreat of *Migtsema*, we need to collect at least one hundred thousand *Migtsema* prayers. After reciting these prayers, we complete our action close retreat by performing at least seven sessions of the *Vajradaka Burning Offering*. In each session we need to collect a hundred Vajradaka mantras together with offerings. This can be done in conjunction with the sadhana in Appendix III.

THE PRACTICE OF THE IN-FRONT-GENERATION

After the mantra recitation in the first three sessions of the day we conclude with the visualization described in the next section, followed by the dedication prayer: 'Through being cared for throughout all my lives ...', see page 147. After the mantra recitation in the last session of the day we bless the tormas and other offerings, and then invite Guru Tsongkhapa together with his retinue to come to the space before us. We strongly believe that Guru Tsongkhapa and all the other Gurus, Yidams, Buddhas, Bodhisattvas, Dakas, Dakinis and Dharma Protectors are actually present in the space in front; and we offer tormas, other offerings and praises in accordance with the words of the sadhana.

CONCLUSION

At the end of each session, all the other holy beings dissolve into Guru Tsongkhapa, who comes to our crown and diminishes to the size of a thumb. He enters our body, descends to our heart, and dissolves into our mind. We strongly believe that inside the central channel at the centre of our heart chakra, on an eight-petalled lotus and moon cushion, is our mind in the form of Je Tsongkhapa who is inseparable from our root Guru. We concentrate single-pointedly on this appearance for a while. Then we imagine that the eight petals of the lotus close together, forming the shape of a heart, without any gaps between the petals. This is completely covered by the letters of the mantra: OM AH RA PA TSA NA DHI SU MA TI KIR TI SHI RI BHA DRA AH

THI TA NA AH THI TI TE KUR BEN TU. To conclude the last session of the day we recite the dedication prayers and auspicious prayers from *King of the Dharma* sadhana.

In summary, the entire practice, from going for refuge up to the auspicious prayers, can be done in conjunction with the *King of the Dharma* sadhana in Appendix III.

THE PRACTICE DURING THE MEDITATION BREAK

Between meditation sessions we should engage in the practices of the meditation break explained previously. In addition we should maintain three special recognitions: (1) that our environment is Tushita Pure Land; (2) that all its inhabitants and enjoyments are pure; and (3) that we are Je Tsongkhapa, the Wisdom Buddha. If we practise this special way of viewing ourself and others, with a pure motivation, it will prevent us from developing delusions such as anger, attachment, jealousy, and so forth, and it will cause us to be reborn in Tushita Pure Land, where we will meet with Je Tsongkhapa's doctrine and eventually become a Wisdom Buddha.

PART TWO

Relying upon the
Dharma Protector

Dorje Shugden

Introduction to the

Dharma Protector

The practice of relying upon the Dharma Protector is explained in five parts:

1 An introduction to the Dharma Protector Dorje Shugden
2 The previous incarnations of Dorje Shugden
3 The nature and function of Dorje Shugden
4 The benefits of relying upon Dorje Shugden
5 The way to rely upon Dorje Shugden

AN INTRODUCTION TO THE DHARMA PROTECTOR DORJE SHUGDEN

A Dharma Protector is an emanation of a Buddha or a Bodhisattva whose main functions are to avert the inner and outer obstacles that prevent practitioners from gaining spiritual realizations, and to arrange all the necessary conditions for their practice. In Tibet, every monastery had its own Dharma Protector, but the tradition did not begin in Tibet; the Mahayanists of ancient India also relied upon Dharma Protectors to eliminate hindrances and to fulfil their spiritual wishes.

Though there are some worldly deities who are friendly towards Buddhism and who try to help practitioners, they are not real Dharma Protectors. Such worldly deities are able to increase the external wealth of practitioners and help them to succeed in their worldly activities, but they do not have the wisdom or the power to protect the development of Dharma within a practitioner's mind. It is this inner Dharma – the experiences of great compassion, bodhichitta, the wisdom realizing emptiness, and so forth – that is most important and that needs to be protected; outer conditions are of secondary importance.

Although their motivation is good, worldly deities lack wisdom and so sometimes the external help that they give actually interferes with the attainment of authentic Dharma realizations. If they have no Dharma realizations themselves, how can they be Dharma Protectors? It is clear therefore that all actual Dharma Protectors must be emanations of Buddhas or Bodhisattvas. These Protectors have great power to protect Buddhadharma and its practitioners, but the extent to which we receive help from them depends upon our faith and conviction in them. To receive their full protection, we must rely upon them with continuous, unwavering devotion.

Buddhas have manifested in the form of various Dharma Protectors, such as Mahakala, Kalarupa, Kalindewi and Dorje Shugden. From the time of Je Tsongkhapa until the first Panchen Lama, Losang Chokyi Gyaltsen, the principal Dharma Protector of Je Tsongkhapa's lineage was Kalarupa. Later, however, it was felt by many high

Lamas that Dorje Shugden had become the principal Dharma Protector of this tradition.

There is no difference in the compassion, wisdom or power of the various Dharma Protectors, but because of the karma of sentient beings, one particular Dharma Protector will have a greater opportunity to help Dharma practitioners at any one particular time. We can understand how this is so by considering the example of Buddha Shakyamuni. Previously the beings of this world had the karma to see Buddha Shakyamuni's Supreme Emanation Body and to receive teachings directly from him. These days, however, we do not have such karma, and so Buddha appears to us in the form of our Spiritual Guide and helps us by giving teachings and leading us on spiritual paths. Thus, the form that Buddha's help takes varies according to our changing karma, but its essential nature remains the same.

Among all the Dharma Protectors, four-faced Mahakala, Kalarupa and Dorje Shugden in particular have the same nature because they are all emanations of Manjushri. However, the beings of this present time have a stronger karmic link with Dorje Shugden than with the other Dharma Protectors. It was for this reason that Morchen Dorjechang Kunga Lhundrup, a very highly realized Master of the Sakya tradition, told his disciples, 'Now is the time to rely upon Dorje Shugden.' He said this on many occasions to encourage his disciples to develop faith in the practice of Dorje Shugden. We too should heed his advice and take it to heart. He did not say that this is the time to rely upon other Dharma Protectors, but clearly stated that now is the time to rely upon Dorje Shugden. Many high Lamas of the Sakya tradition and many Sakya monasteries have relied sincerely upon Dorje Shugden.

In recent years the person most responsible for propagating the practice of Dorje Shugden was the late Vajradhara Trijang Rinpoche, the root Guru of many Gelugpa practitioners from humble novices to the highest Lamas. He encouraged all his disciples to rely upon Dorje Shugden and gave Dorje Shugden empowerments many times. Even in his old age, so as to prevent the practice of Dorje Shugden from degenerating he wrote an extensive text entitled *Symphony Delighting an Ocean of Conquerors*, which is a commentary to Tagpo Kelsang Khedrub Rinpoche's praise of Dorje Shugden called *Infinite Aeons*.

Previous Incarnations of the
Dharma Protector

THE PREVIOUS INCARNATIONS OF DORJE SHUGDEN

The highly realized Master, Tagpo Kelsang Khedrub Rinpoche, composed the following two verses concerning Dorje Shugden:

> With deep faith I prostrate to you, Vajradhara Dorje
>   Shugden.
> Although you have already attained the Buddha
>   ground
> And engage in the twenty-seven deeds of a Buddha,
> You appear in various forms to help the
>   Buddhadharma and living beings.
>
> You have manifested in different aspects
> As Indian and Tibetan Masters,
> Such as Manjushri, Mahasiddha Biwawa, Sakya
>   Pandita,
> Buton Rinchen Drub, Duldzin Dragpa Gyaltsen,
>   Panchen Sonam Dragpa, and many others.

The five lineages of Dorje Shugden

The meaning of the first verse is quite clear. The twenty-seven deeds of a Buddha are explained in the *Perfection of Wisdom Sutras* and in the eighth chapter of Maitreya's *Ornament for Clear Realization*. These twenty-seven deeds range from showing living beings the way to enter the spiritual path to liberation up to guiding them to the final attainment of Buddhahood. Since Dorje Shugden performs all these twenty-seven deeds it is clear that he is a Buddha.

To guide living beings along the spiritual path, Dorje Shugden manifests many different aspects. Sometimes he appears in a peaceful aspect, sometimes in a wrathful aspect, sometimes as an ordained person, sometimes as a lay person, sometimes as a Bodhisattva, sometimes as a Hinayanist, sometimes as a non-Buddhist, and sometimes even as a non-human being. Since there are so many different emanations of the Buddhas, it is difficult to tell who is an emanation and who is not. The only person we can be certain about is ourself; we know whether we are a living being or a Buddha, but we do not know about others.

Each Buddha has the ability to manifest as many emanations as there are living beings. This ability is necessary because if Buddhas remained in only one form, without any emanations, they would not be able to help all living beings according to their different needs. Thus, if we refuse to believe that a Buddha can have many different emanations we are indirectly holding the wrong view of denying that Buddhas can help all living beings. In *Meeting of Father and Son Sutra* Buddha Shakyamuni says:

Buddhas manifest in many different aspects such as Brahma, Indra, and sometimes even as a mara or in the aspect of an evil person – but worldly people do not recognize these emanations.

Buddhas can emanate even as inanimate objects. At one time, the great Indian Master, Phadampa Sangye, journeyed to Tibet. When Milarepa heard of this great Yogi's visit he decided to test his realizations. He went to the border and waited for Phadampa Sangye to arrive. When he saw him approaching he transformed himself into a flower to see whether Phadampa Sangye had the clairvoyance to see through his disguise. Phadampa Sangye, however, walked straight past Milarepa, seemingly unaware of his presence. Milarepa thought to himself, 'This so-called Yogi has no clairvoyance', whereupon Phadampa Sangye turned round and kicked the flower. 'Get up Milarepa!' he said, and Milarepa, delighted to discover that Phadampa Sangye was a genuinely realized being, sprang up in his usual form to greet him.

As Tagpo Kelsang Khedrub Rinpoche said, Dorje Shugden has manifested in many different forms to help living beings. There now follows a brief account of each of the past incarnations of Dorje Shugden mentioned in the verse quoted above.

MANJUSHRI

At the time of Buddha Shakyamuni, Dorje Shugden appeared as the Bodhisattva Manjushri, one of Buddha's principal disciples. In reality Manjushri had already attained full enlightenment in a previous age, long before the time of Buddha Shakyamuni. In *Sutra Revealing the Abode of Manjushri* Buddha explains that in the remote past Manjushri had completed the Bodhisattva path and attained enlightenment in his Pure Land as a Buddha called 'Tathagata Lamp of the Nagas'. In the same Sutra Buddha also describes the many different Buddha Lands of Manjushri, and how Manjushri manifests countless emanations to help living beings.

Although Manjushri showed the aspect of being a disciple of Buddha, he had great power to help living beings. Sometimes people would come to Buddha for help and advice but Buddha would refer them to Manjushri because they had a stronger karmic link with him. Some had such a strong connection with Manjushri that, through his blessings and skill, they were able to develop very powerful realizations with almost no effort on their part.

One such person was King Ajatashatru, who had committed two particularly negative actions – killing his father and raping a fully ordained nun who was also a Superior being. The consequences of such actions are horrendous. In the *Vinaya Sutras* such actions are called 'actions of immediate retribution' because whoever commits them will definitely take rebirth in a hell realm immediately after his or her death. According to the *Vinaya Sutras* it is impossible to prevent such a rebirth, although it may be possible to shorten its duration. According to the Mahayana Sutras, however, these heavy negative actions can be purified if the correct opponents are applied purely.

King Ajatashatru developed strong remorse for his negative actions and requested Buddha to give him a special method for purifying them. Buddha taught *Sutra for Eliminating Ajatashatru's Regret* and then suggested that the king seek the help of Bodhisattva Manjushri. Immediately upon hearing this advice, Ajatashatru developed strong faith in Manjushri. He invited Manjushri to his house for a banquet, and after the meal he rose to offer Manjushri a very expensive cloak; but just as he was presenting the garment Manjushri disappeared. The king was left wondering, 'Who is Manjushri? Where is Manjushri?' By thinking in this way he realized that he could not find a real, truly existent Manjushri, and he came very close to understanding emptiness. Since Manjushri had disappeared, the king decided to try the cloak on himself; but as he put it round his shoulders he started asking the same questions about himself, 'Who am I? Where am I? Who is the king? Where is the king?' Being completely unable to find a real, truly existent self or truly existent king, he gained an understanding of emptiness. He then entered into meditation and quickly attained a direct realization of emptiness, becoming a Superior being on the path of seeing.

According to the Hinayana teachings, a person who has committed one of the five actions of immediate retribution cannot become a Superior being in that same life, but the Mahayana viewpoint is different. As a result of Manjushri's blessings, King Ajatashatru was able to purify his heavy negative karma and attain the path of seeing. Manjushri performed many other special actions such as this.

MAHASIDDHA BIWAWA

Later, to help the Buddhadharma flourish, Manjushri took rebirth as the Mahasiddha Biwawa. Biwawa was born in India, to the east of Bodh Gaya, and joined Nalanda Monastery at a young age. Although he was an emanation of Manjushri and therefore a fully enlightened being, Biwawa studied and practised Buddha's teachings at Nalanda so as to demonstrate a perfect example of how to practise the path to liberation and enlightenment. During the day he studied and meditated on the Sutra teachings, and during the night he practised the yogas of *Heruka Tantra*. As a result of his pure practice he was able to see Vajrayogini and her retinue directly. Whenever he made tsog offerings, Vajrayogini together with fifteen other Dakinis with whom he had a particularly strong karmic connection would come to his room to participate in the feast.

Unfortunately the other monks at Nalanda did not recognize Vajrayogini and the Dakinis but saw them as ordinary women. Believing that he was breaking his ordination vows, they became very critical of him and nicknamed him 'Biwawa', which means 'bad man'. Thinking that Biwawa's behaviour gave the monastery a bad reputation, they asked him to leave. Although Biwawa had never broken any of his Vinaya vows, he agreed to leave Nalanda, saying, 'Yes, I am a bad man, I will leave.' He handed back his robes, changed into lay clothes, and left the monastery. Then, just like a poor, homeless beggar he began wandering from place to place.

He first went to an area near Varanasi and lived in a cave deep in the forest. The land belonged to a non-Buddhist king who had an intense hatred of Buddhists. One day the king met Biwawa and invited him back to the palace, but when he learnt that Biwawa was a Buddhist he ordered his servants to kill him. The servants first tried drowning Biwawa, but they were unable to pick him up to throw him into the river. They then tried to bury him alive, but he reappeared the next day unharmed. Finally they tried to burn him to death, but again he emerged unharmed. When the king saw that Biwawa was able to protect himself through his miracle powers, he developed strong faith in him and in the Buddhadharma, and he and all his subjects became Buddhist practitioners and disciples of Biwawa. This fulfilled a prediction made by an astrologer at the time of Biwawa's birth that Biwawa would become very powerful and, through demonstrating miracle powers, would cause many people to enter the Buddhadharma.

Sometime later Biwawa travelled south to the River Ganges. When he arrived at the river he asked a ferryman to take him across, but the ferryman refused because Biwawa had no money with which to pay him. Biwawa declared, 'Since this river flows continuously, perhaps it is tired and would like a rest' and, causing the waters to part, he walked across to the other side. The ferryman was astounded and asked Biwawa who he was. Biwawa told him a little of his life story, whereupon the ferryman developed great faith and asked to become one of his disciples. Biwawa accepted him as a disciple and gave him many teachings. The ferryman practised diligently and eventually became a highly realized Yogi called Drombi Heruka, one of the eighty-four Mahasiddhas.

Continuing on his travels, Biwawa reached a town where he stopped at the local tavern. After he had consumed several drinks the landlady asked him to pay, but Biwawa replied that he had no money. The landlady became angry and threatened him, 'You have until sunset to pay me, otherwise I will call the authorities and have you thrown into jail!' Biwawa promptly used his miracle powers to stop the sun moving and held it motionless for three whole days. The local people were aghast and wondered how such a thing could happen. Finally they asked the king to help them. When the king asked Biwawa what was happening, Biwawa replied that he was responsible for the sun not setting. 'If I allow the sun to set,' he explained, 'I will have to go to jail.' The king then reassured Biwawa that if he allowed the sun to set he would not have to pay for his drinks or go to jail. Upon hearing of his reprieve, Biwawa was delighted and immediately allowed the sun to continue its journey across the sky!

As a result of Biwawa's extraordinary deeds, many people developed faith in him and in Buddhadharma. In this way, he led many people into the spiritual path. When the monks at Nalanda heard of his activities, they developed great regret at having expelled him and requested him to return to the monastery, but Biwawa declined their invitation.

The nine Great Mothers

SAKYA PANDITA

Biwawa later took rebirth in western Tibet as the great Lama of the Sakya Tradition, Sachen Kunga Gyaltsen, more usually known as Sakya Pandita. Even ordinary beings recognized that he was a very special being. When he was a young child, the first language he spoke was not Tibetan but Sanskrit, even though he had never been taught it. He was able to memorize texts even during his dreams. For example, he once dreamt that the great Indian Pandit Vasubandhu was giving him teachings on his text *Treasury of Abhidharma*, and when he awoke he had memorized the entire text, which is almost fifty pages long. Following his Guru, Jetsun Dragpa Gyaltsen, Sakya Pandita studied and practised both Sutra and Tantra and became a great scholar and meditator who was famous for his wisdom and miracle powers.

Sakya Pandita's name spread far and wide, reaching even the Chinese Emperor. The Emperor took a keen interest in Sakya Pandita and invited him to China so that he could meet him in person. He decided to use the visit as an opportunity to check whether or not Sakya Pandita was actually enlightened. He summoned a highly qualified magician and told him to emanate a beautiful palace, together with servants, magnificent ornaments, and decorations. Such magicians were very different from those we have nowadays in the West. Through a combination of their concentration, mantra recitation, and special substances they could emanate houses, or even whole cities, for days or months. Unfortunately they did not have the powers to maintain their magical creations indefinitely, and after a while the emanations would disappear. For the duration of their existence, however, their emanations seemed to be real, and people would live in them without ever suspecting that they were magically created illusions. The Emperor thought that if Sakya Pandita really was enlightened he would not be fooled by such an emanated palace, but if he was just an ordinary person he would probably think that it was real.

When Sakya Pandita arrived in China, the Emperor took him to the emanated palace and asked him what he thought of it, and Sakya Pandita replied that it was very beautiful. 'Do you think this is a real palace?' enquired the Emperor, 'Yes', replied Sakya Pandita, 'Of course it is real.' From this reply the Emperor concluded that Sakya Pandita was not actually a Buddha but just an ordinary being who was deceiving the people of Tibet and China. The Emperor then commanded the magician to re-absorb his emanation, but when he tried to do so he found that he could not. Unbeknown to the Emperor and the magician, Sakya Pandita had used his own miracle powers to transform the emanated palace into a real one! When he discovered this, the Emperor was filled with remorse for having had such negative thoughts about Sakya Pandita. He immediately developed strong faith in him and became one of his disciples. It is said that the palace still exists today as a temple known as 'The Emanation Temple'.

BUTON RINCHEN DRUB

Sakya Pandita later took rebirth as Buton Rinchen Drub. He was born in western Tibet near the place where Tashilhunpo Monastery now stands, and was ordained as a monk at an early age. Even while he was a young child his parents realized that he was a very special being. The child would often converse with Manjushri as naturally as he would talk with other people, and it was clear from his speech and his actions that he had already attained great compassion and bodhichitta.

Although Buton did not put much effort into learning Sanskrit, he was able to understand it with great ease. He translated Sanskrit texts not previously translated into Tibetan and he corrected many earlier translations. He became a very great and famous Lama, a learned scholar who was wise in both Sutra and Tantra, and he wrote twenty-six volumes of extensive commentaries on subjects from the Kangyur and the Tengyur. Buton's works are so vast that it is difficult for ordinary people to see them as a whole and determine their essential meaning, but they can be clearly understood by following Je Tsongkhapa's elucidations. Buton's works and Je Tsongkhapa's works are very closely related. It is said that if you want to know many different things you should read Buton's books, and if you want to come to definite conclusions you should read the works of Je Tsongkhapa.

Buton mainly emphasized the need to practise Buddhadharma purely. He demonstrated fewer miracle powers than previous incarnations, spending most of his time teaching and writing. At the time of Manjushri and Mahasiddha Biwawa, people generally had more merit and much purer minds, and so displays of miracle powers were often very powerful and effective in causing them to develop faith and other realizations. As times became more degenerate, however, people had less merit and their minds were less pure. For them, displays of miracle powers tended to be counter-productive, giving rise to doubts, scepticism, jealousy and other negative minds rather than pure minds such as faith. People would even suspect those who displayed miracle powers of using them for selfish or political ends, and those who had dark inner secrets would be fearful of their being exposed. In such situations, those who displayed miracle powers would sometimes find themselves in danger of their lives. Moreover, there would be a danger that they would attract only disciples who craved miracle powers for themselves. It was for these reasons that Je Tsongkhapa later forbade his disciples to display their miracle powers. The later incarnations of Manjushri, therefore, placed less and less emphasis on miracle powers, choosing instead to help living beings by setting a perfect example and giving clear and precise instructions on the path to enlightenment. Thus, realized beings such as Sakya Pandita and Buton Rinchen Drub showed practitioners how to meditate correctly and how to gain experience of the stages of the path, leading them to profound realizations of concentration and wisdom. In this way, they tamed the deluded minds of their disciples and led them out of suffering and into pure happiness.

DULDZIN DRAGPA GYALTSEN

Buton Rinchen Drub was later reborn in central Tibet as Duldzin Dragpa Gyaltsen, who became one of Je Tsongkhapa's principal disciples. Like Je Tsongkhapa he was a very pure practitioner of the Vinaya and so he was called 'Duldzin', which is short for 'dulwa dzinpa', or 'Holder of the Vinaya'.

Although Duldzin showed the aspect of being a disciple of Je Tsongkhapa, he was in fact an emanation of Manjushri. Thus, both Teacher and disciple were emanations of Manjushri. From the point of view of ordinary beings this may seem a contradiction but in reality it is not. When he was teaching the Sutras and Tantras, Buddha would sometimes manifest as both the Teacher and the principal interlocutors who helped the discourse to evolve. In one of the Tantras, Buddha Vajradhara said, 'I am the Teacher and I am the disciple. I am the speaker and I am the listener.' There are Tantras that were requested by Vajrapani, who was an emanation of Vajradhara; and often among the audience there were many other emanations. Since Manjushri is a Buddha, he can also manifest countless emanations simultaneously, and so it is not impossible that both Je Tsongkhapa and Duldzin Dragpa Gyaltsen were his emanations.

Duldzin Dragpa Gyaltsen's main activity was to help the teachings of Je Tsongkhapa to flourish. He worked to remove obstacles and to gather favourable conditions for the dissemination of these precious teachings. It was Je Tsongkhapa's wish that the special Dharma derived from

Manjushri's wisdom should spread far and wide, and Duldzin, as his devoted disciple, worked tirelessly to fulfil his Guru's wish.

Je Tsongkhapa travelled extensively in response to invitations to give teachings, and also engaged in profound retreats for the purposes of writing and meditating; and while he was away he would leave Duldzin in charge of his affairs. It was Duldzin Dragpa Gyaltsen, for example, who organized the building of Ganden Monastery.

Rather than demonstrating miracle powers, Duldzin demonstrated how to practise pure Dharma by relying sincerely upon his Spiritual Guide, maintaining pure moral discipline, and so forth. Like Je Tsongkhapa he showed that there is no contradiction between the external practices of Vinaya, the internal practices of the Bodhisattva path, and the secret practices of the generation and completion stages of Highest Yoga Tantra.

Je Tsongkhapa's disciples believed that Duldzin Dragpa Gyaltsen and Je Tsongkhapa were equal in terms of their realizations, abilities and wisdom. When Je Tsongkhapa passed away, his throne was offered first to Duldzin, but Duldzin declined the honour and offered it instead to Gyaltsabje, saying, 'You should become the second holder of the Ganden throne. You should teach the Dharma of Je Tsongkhapa and spread it far and wide. I will help your work to be successful by eliminating obstacles and arranging the right conditions.'

PANCHEN SONAM DRAGPA

Duldzin Dragpa Gyaltsen was later reborn in central Tibet and became a special Lama known as Panchen Sonam Dragpa. Like Duldzin, he worked to remove obstacles to the flourishing of Je Tsongkhapa's tradition and to gather conducive conditions.

This Lama was unique in that at different times in his life he became the Abbot of Gyuto Tantric College, Ganden Monastery, Drepung Monastery and Sera Monastery; and while he was Abbot of Ganden Monastery he also became the fifteenth holder of Je Tsongkhapa's throne. In those days the Abbots were elected by the resident monks, and the high esteem in which Panchen Sonam Dragpa was held was demonstrated by his having been appointed Abbot of all four principal monasteries. He is the only person ever to have received this honour.

Panchen Sonam Dragpa wrote many commentaries to both Sutra and Tantra. To this day at Drepung Loseling, the largest Gelugpa monastery, as well as at Ganden Shartse, monks qualify for their Geshe degrees by relying principally upon the works of this great Teacher. He is also highly regarded at other monasteries, such as Sera.

Throughout his life, Panchen Sonam Dragpa worked to further Je Tsongkhapa's doctrine. When he became holder of Je Tsongkhapa's throne, he composed the following prayer:

So that the tradition of Je Tsongkhapa,
The King of the Dharma, may flourish,
May all obstacles be pacified
And may all favourable conditions abound.

Some time later, when he attended the Monlam Chenmo, or Great Prayer Festival, founded by Je Tsongkhapa, he composed a special verse of dedication:

Through the two collections of myself and others
Gathered throughout the three times,
May the doctrine of Conqueror Losang Dragpa
Flourish for evermore.

These prayers, which are recited every day after teachings and pujas at all Gelugpa monasteries and Dharma Centres, indicate that Panchen Sonam Dragpa's activities were the same as Dorje Shugden's – working to cause Je Tsongkhapa's doctrine to flourish.

Later in life Panchen Sonam Dragpa became the Spiritual Guide of the reincarnation of the first Dalai Lama, Je Gendundrub, granting him ordination and giving him the name Sonam Gyatso. It was Sonam Gyatso who visited Mongolia and so impressed the ruler, Altan Khan, that both he and his subjects were converted to Buddhism. The Khan gave him the title 'Dalai Lama', which in Mongolian means 'Ocean Lama'. Although he was the first to be so called, he became known as the third Dalai Lama, his two previous incarnations, Je Gendundrub and Je Gendun Gyatso, acquiring posthumously the titles of first and second Dalai Lama.

When Panchen Sonam Dragpa died he remained in single-pointed concentration on the clear light of death for fifteen days. His body then diminished to the size of a forearm and from this body many statues and relics appeared. From his manner of dying we can understand clearly that he had attained the illusory body and was truly an enlightened being.

NGATRUL DRAGPA GYALTSEN

Ngatrul Dragpa Gyaltsen was the reincarnation of Panchen Sonam Dragpa. He lived at Drepung Monastery at the same time as the fifth Dalai Lama, and both these Lamas were disciples of the first Panchen Lama, Losang Chokyi Gyaltsen.

Ngatrul Dragpa Gyaltsen studied both Sutra and Tantra, mainly under the first Panchen Lama, and became a great scholar and meditator. He was highly respected and considered to be a very pure and precious Teacher. Meditating in over a hundred caves, he received many direct visions of Buddhas, Bodhisattvas and Deities. He made a number of predictions, including one that he would become Dorje Shugden. Ngatrul Dragpa Gyaltsen died at a relatively young age.

The eight Fully Ordained Monks

The Nature and Function of the
Dharma Protector

THE NATURE AND FUNCTION OF DORJE SHUGDEN

Dorje Shugden and the Deities of his mandala are the same nature as the Deities of the body mandala of Lama Losang Tubwang Dorjechang, who is in essence Je Tsongkhapa. After Je Tsongkhapa passed away, Khedrubje received five visions of him, each time appearing in a different aspect. Later the great Yogi Dharmavajra saw Je Tsongkhapa in the aspect of Lama Losang Tubwang Dorjechang. This name was given to Je Tsongkhapa by Manjushri. It indicates that Je Tsongkhapa is the embodiment of both Conqueror Vajradhara and Buddha Shakyamuni. 'Losang Dragpa' is Je Tsongkhapa's ordained name, 'Tubwang' or 'Powerful Able One' is an epithet of Buddha Shakyamuni, and 'Dorjechang' is Tibetan for Vajradhara. Lama Losang Tubwang Dorjechang is an enlightened being and the principal Field for Accumulating Merit in the Guru yoga of *Offering to the Spiritual Guide*, or *Lama Chopa*.

In reality the *Lama Chopa* instruction comes from Manjushri's *Emanation Scripture*, which includes special instructions on Mahamudra. The *Emanation Scripture,* which cannot be read by ordinary beings, was revealed directly to Je Tsongkhapa by Manjushri. It was passed down to successive lineage Gurus, and when it reached the first Panchen Lama, Losang Chokyi Gyaltsen, he extracted the instructions on *Lama Chopa* and *Root Text of the Mahamudra, the Main Path of the Conquerors* and wrote them down in Tibetan. This was an act of great kindness because it meant that for the first time ordinary beings could read and practise *Lama Chopa* and the special close lineage of Vajrayana Mahamudra. The Guru yoga of *Lama Chopa* is one of the most blessed practices within Je Tsongkhapa's tradition, being the essential preliminary practice for Vajrayana Mahamudra. An extensive commentary to this practice can be found in the book *Great Treasury of Merit*.

There are thirty-two Deities within the body mandala of Lama Losang Tubwang Dorjechang, and it is these Deities who manifest as the thirty-two Deities of Dorje Shugden's mandala. This was explained by Je Phabongkhapa, an emanation of Heruka, in his prayer to Dorje Shugden:

The aggregates, elements, sources and limbs of
    Lama Losang Tubwang Dorjechang
Appear in the aspect of the five lineages of Dorje
    Shugden and their retinues.
Realizing that in reality I am practising the yoga of
    the thirty-two Deities of the body mandala,
I offer this practice to you, O Five lineages of Dorje
    Shugden; please accept it with delight.

The way the thirty-two Deities of Dorje Shugden's mandala relate to the Deities of Lama Losang Tubwang

Dorjechang's body mandala is shown in the chart in Appendix II.

Of the Deities of the five lineages of Dorje Shugden, the principal Deity is Duldzin Dorje Shugden. He is a manifestation of the aggregate of consciousness of Lama Losang Tubwang Dorjechang. Vairochana Shugden is a manifestation of the form aggregate of Lama Losang Tubwang Dorjechang, Ratna Shugden is a manifestation of his aggregate of feeling, Pema Shugden is a manifestation of his aggregate of discrimination and Karma Shugden is a manifestation of his aggregate of compositional factors.

Many sadhanas of Dorje Shugden state that Dorje Shugden is the embodiment of the 'Guru, Yidam and Protector'. Here, 'Guru' refers specifically to Lama Tsongkhapa. Thus, when we practise the sadhana of Dorje Shugden we are indirectly practising the Guru yoga of Je Tsongkhapa, as well as the practices of Yamantaka and Kalarupa. Atisha used to say, 'Some of you Tibetans have tried to accomplish a hundred Deities but have failed to gain a single attainment, while some Indian Buddhists have gained the attainments of a hundred Deities by accomplishing the practice of just one.' We should bear Atisha's comment in mind and realize that it is much more meaningful to practise one Deity sincerely, regarding that Deity as the synthesis of all Deities, than it is to practise many Deities superficially.

Some people believe that Dorje Shugden is an emanation of Manjushri who shows the aspect of a worldly being, but this is incorrect. Even Dorje Shugden's form reveals the complete stages of the path of Sutra and Tantra, and such qualities are not possessed by the forms of worldly beings. Dorje Shugden appears as a fully ordained monk to show that the practice of pure moral discipline is essential for those who wish to attain enlightenment. In his left hand he holds a heart, which symbolizes great compassion and spontaneous great bliss – the essence of all the stages of the vast path of Sutra and Tantra. His round yellow hat represents the view of Nagarjuna, and the wisdom sword in his right hand teaches us to sever ignorance, the root of samsara, with the sharp blade of Nagarjuna's view. This is the essence of all the stages of the profound path of Sutra and Tantra.

Dorje Shugden rides a snow lion, the symbol of the four fearlessnesses of a Buddha, and has a jewel-spitting mongoose perched on his left arm, symbolizing his power to bestow wealth on those who put their trust in him. The single eye in the centre of his forehead symbolizes his omniscient wisdom, which perceives directly and simultaneously all past, present and future phenomena. His wrathful expression indicates that he destroys ignorance, the real enemy of all living beings, by blessing them with great wisdom; and also that he destroys the obstacles of pure Dharma practitioners.

Each of the thirty-two Deities of Dorje Shugden's mandala has a specific function, which are explained in a prayer written by Sachen Kunlo, one of the great Sakya Lamas. In this prayer he explains that the function of Duldzin Dorje Shugden, the principal Deity of the mandala, is to lead faithful followers to correct spiritual paths by bestowing great wisdom; the function of Vairochana Shugden is to help us to pacify our negative karma and obstacles; the function of Ratna Shugden is to help us to increase our good fortune, life span and virtuous realizations; the function of Pema Shugden is to help us to control our own mind so that we can help others achieve controlled, calm and peaceful states of mind; and the function of Karma Shugden is to overcome the four maras and evil spirits who try to harm faithful disciples. The nine Great Mothers help faithful followers of Dorje Shugden in their Tantric practices, the eight Fully Ordained Monks help them in their practices of Sutra, and the ten Wrathful Deities aid them in their various daily activities. In these spiritually degenerate times, Dharma practitioners experience many obstacles, but if we rely upon Dorje Shugden with unwavering faith he will care for us just like a father caring for his children.

In general, all Buddhist practitioners need to develop unwavering faith in Buddha Shakyamuni, for without it their Dharma practice will have little power and bring few results; and in particular all Gelugpa practitioners need to develop firm and lasting faith in Je Tsongkhapa, otherwise they will never experience the unique qualities of his doctrine. Faith is the very root of all Dharma experience. Gelugpa practitioners who have a sincere trust in Dorje Shugden will have no difficulty in generating unshakeable faith in Je Tsongkhapa. Their practice of view, meditation and action will naturally become pure, and they will easily realize the special uncommon qualities of Je Tsongkhapa's teachings. Thus, they will be able to gain experience of the stages of the path of both Sutra and Tantra without any difficulty.

THE BENEFITS OF RELYING UPON DORJE SHUGDEN

If we can understand well the nature and functions of Dorje Shugden, we can understand the benefits of relying upon him. Dorje Shugden always helps, guides and protects pure and faithful practitioners by granting blessings, increasing their wisdom, fulfilling their wishes, and bestowing success on all their virtuous activities. Dorje Shugden does not help only Gelugpas; because he is a Buddha he helps all living beings, including non-Buddhists. The sun benefits even those born blind, giving them warmth and ripening the crops that become their food; but should they gain their sight, how much more obvious its benefit would be! In a similar way, although Dorje Shugden protects even those who do not make an effort to rely upon him, when our eyes of faith in him open and we rely upon him sincerely we will gradually become more aware of the help we receive from him. If we sincerely wish to experience the benefits of relying upon Dorje Shugden, we must rely upon him constantly over a long period of time, steadily improving our connection with him. In this way, we will begin to notice his beneficial influence in our lives.

We should understand that the principal function of a Dharma Protector is to protect our Dharma practice, not to help our mundane affairs. Bearing this in mind we should not become discouraged if we do not suddenly become very wealthy, for wealth does not necessarily help spiritual practice and can be a great distraction. If we rely sincerely upon Dorje Shugden, he will arrange the conditions that are most conducive for our Dharma practice but these will not necessarily be the ones that we ourself would have chosen! Dorje Shugden will bless our minds to help us transform difficult situations into the spiritual path, and he will open the wisdom eyes of his faithful followers, enabling them always to make the right decisions. Although physically they may find themselves alone, inwardly those who put their trust in him will never be apart from a powerful ally and a wise and compassionate guide.

One Lama called Gyara Tulku Rinpoche from Drepung Loseling Monastery wrote a prayer to Dorje Shugden expressing his gratitude. In this prayer, he said:

First you gave me a highly qualified Spiritual Guide
Under whom I studied and practised Dharma.
When through following misleading advice I came
    close to entering wrong paths,
You immediately hooked me back into the correct
    path.

This Lama spent many years in a country where he did not even know the language and where conditions were very difficult. However, he became highly respected and many people sought his wise counsel. He realized that all his spiritual progress, happiness, health and success came from Dorje Shugden and not from himself. In the same prayer, he wrote:

O Duldzin, King of the Dharma, I thank you for
    your kindness.
Your body is the synthesis of all Sangha Jewels,
Your speech is the synthesis of all Dharma Jewels,
And your mind is the synthesis of all Buddha Jewels.

The ten Wrathful Deities

The Way to Rely upon the Dharma Protector

The way to rely upon Dorje Shugden has two parts:

1 The way to rely upon Dorje Shugden in thought and deed
2 The way to practise the sadhana of Dorje Shugden

THE WAY TO RELY UPON DORJE SHUGDEN IN THOUGHT AND DEED

There are two ways to rely upon Dorje Shugden: in thought and in deed. If we recognize that Dorje Shugden is the embodiment of the Three Jewels, if we remember his kindness in protecting and preserving the Buddhadharma, if we recall how he eliminates obstacles and gathers the necessary conditions for Dharma practitioners, and if with deep faith we develop respect for him and hold these special feelings continually, we are relying upon Dorje Shugden in thought.

With deep faith and conviction in Dorje Shugden, we can practise his extensive, middling or condensed sadhana. After completing a close retreat we can engage in peaceful, increasing, controlling and wrathful actions and gradually accomplish the supreme attainments. By engaging in these practices we can protect others by helping them to eliminate their obstacles and develop wisdom, to find the right conditions for practising Dharma, to fulfil their wishes, and to meet with success in their daily lives. Whenever we engage in any of these deeds with faith, we are relying upon Dorje Shugden in deed.

There are many commentaries, rituals, and sadhanas in relation to Dorje Shugden that were composed by high Sakya and Gelugpa Lamas. For beings of this present age, the late Vajradhara Trijang Rinpoche, who was the embodiment of Buddha Shakyamuni, Heruka, Atisha and Je Tsongkhapa, wrote his great commentary to *Infinite Aeons*, the praise to Dorje Shugden composed by Tagpo Kelsang Khedrub Rinpoche. He also wrote many special rituals and yogas for gaining different attainments connected with Dorje Shugden. Through his great kindness, and by following his writings, I have had the opportunity to write this short commentary on Dorje Shugden.

THE WAY TO PRACTISE THE SADHANA OF DORJE SHUGDEN

There are common sadhanas and special sadhanas of Dorje Shugden. The common sadhanas, such as the *Heart Jewel* sadhana, can be practised by anyone who has faith, regardless of whether or not they have received a Highest Yoga Tantra empowerment or a blessing empowerment of Dorje Shugden. We begin by practising *The Hundreds of Deities of the Joyful Land*, which is the first part of the

Heart Jewel sadhana, up to dissolving Guru Tsongkhapa into our heart and reciting the dedication prayers. This practice helps us to make a strong connection with Dorje Shugden. After this we recite the common sadhana of Dorje Shugden, with which we make offerings and requests for the elimination of obstacles, and we pray to achieve whatever conditions we need for our practice and for the Buddhadharma to flourish.

If we have received a Highest Yoga Tantra empowerment, we can practise uncommon sadhanas, such as the *Wishfulfilling Jewel* sadhana found in Appendix III. Having practised *The Hundreds of Deities of the Joyful Land* and absorbed the Guru into our heart, we should generate ourself as our Yidam, invite Dorje Shugden, and then make offerings and requests according to the words of the sadhana.

In conclusion, we need to recognize that all Buddha's wisdom appears in the aspect of Manjushri, that he in turn appears in the aspect of Je Tsongkhapa, and that he in turn appears as Dorje Shugden. Keeping this recognition in mind we should develop and maintain unchangeable faith in Buddha, Manjushri, Je Tsongkhapa and Dorje Shugden.

Dedication

Through my virtues from composing this book with
pure motivation,
May all living beings, throughout all their lives,
Never be parted from peaceful and wrathful
Manjushri,
But always come under their care.

Appendix I:

The Condensed Meaning of the

Commentary

The Condensed Meaning of the Commentary

The commentary to the sadhana *Heart Jewel*, the essential practices of Kadampa Buddhism, has three parts:

1 The instruction of the Guru yoga of Je Tsongkhapa according to the Segyu lineage
2 Relying upon the Dharma Protector
3 Dedication

The instruction of the Guru yoga of Je Tsongkhapa according to the Segyu lineage has two parts:

1 Introduction
2 The actual practice of the instruction

The introduction has three parts:

1 Je Tsongkhapa
2 The history and lineage of the instruction
3 The benefits of this practice

The actual practice of the instruction has three parts:

1 The actual practice
2 An explanation of the *Migtsema* prayer
3 How to do a close retreat of *Migtsema*

The actual practice has two parts:

1 The practice during the meditation session
2 The practice during the meditation break

The practice during the meditation session has five parts:

1 The preliminary practices of going for refuge and generating bodhichitta
2 Inviting the Field for Accumulating Merit
3 Accumulating merit
4 Receiving attainments by making requests
5 Conclusion

The preliminary practices of going for refuge and generating bodhichitta has four parts:

1 The objects of refuge
2 Generating the causes of going for refuge
3 The prayer of going for refuge
4 Generating bodhichitta

Accumulating merit has eight parts:

1 Requesting the Spiritual Guide to remain for a long time
2 Prostration
3 Offering
4 Purification
5 Rejoicing
6 Requesting the turning of the Wheel of Dharma
7 Dedication
8 Offering the mandala

Receiving attainments by making requests has two parts:

1 Making requests
2 Receiving attainments

Making requests has three parts:

1 Making requests with regard to Je Tsongkhapa's outer qualities
2 Making requests with regard to Je Tsongkhapa's inner qualities
3 Making requests with regard to Je Tsongkhapa's secret qualities

Receiving attainments has two parts:

1 Purifying impurities
2 Accomplishing wisdom and attaining the realizations of the stages of the path

Accomplishing wisdom and attaining the realizations of the stages of the path has two parts:

1 Accomplishing wisdom
2 Attaining the realizations of the stages of the path

Accomplishing wisdom has two parts:

1 An introduction to the seven types of wisdom
2 The actual practice

An introduction to the seven types of wisdom has seven parts:

1 Great wisdom
2 Clear wisdom

3 Quick wisdom

4 Profound wisdom

5 The wisdom of expounding Dharma

6 The wisdom of spiritual debate

7 The wisdom of composing Dharma books

The actual practice has seven parts:

1 Receiving the attainment of great wisdom

2 Receiving the attainment of clear wisdom

3 Receiving the attainment of quick wisdom

4 Receiving the attainment of profound wisdom

5 Receiving the attainment of the wisdom of expounding Dharma

6 Receiving the attainment of the wisdom of spiritual debate

7 Receiving the attainment of the wisdom of composing Dharma books

An explanation of the *Migtsema* prayer has two parts:

1 An explanation of the first line

2 An explanation of the remaining four lines

An explanation of the first line has three parts:

1 With regard to the pre-eminent qualities of his teachings, Je Tsongkhapa is unequalled among all Tibetan scholars

2 With regard to his practical example, Je Tsongkhapa is unequalled among all Tibetan scholars

3 With regard to his Dharma activities, Je Tsongkhapa is unequalled among all Tibetan scholars

How to do a close retreat of *Migtsema* has four parts:

1 What is a retreat?
2 The necessary conditions for a close retreat of
   Migtsema
3 The preparations for a close retreat of *Migtsema*
4 The practice of an action close retreat of *Migtsema*

The practice of an action close retreat of *Migtsema* has two parts:

1 The practice during the meditation session
2 The practice during the meditation break

The practice during the meditation session has three parts:

1 Preliminary practices
2 The actual practice
3 Conclusion

The actual practice has six parts:

1 Purifying our body and mind by meditating on
   emptiness
2 Transforming the basis of imputation for our I by
   generating ourself as Guru Tsongkhapa
3 Meditating on divine pride
4 Meditating on clear appearance
5 Reciting the mantras
6 The practice of the in-front-generation

Transforming the basis of imputation for our I by
generating ourself as Guru Tsongkhapa has four parts:

1 What is the basis of imputation for our I?

2 Why we need to change the basis of imputation for our I

3 How it is possible to change the basis of imputation for our I

4 How to change the basis of imputation for our I

Relying upon the Dharma Protector has five parts:

1 An introduction to the Dharma Protector Dorje Shugden

2 The previous incarnations of Dorje Shugden

3 The nature and function of Dorje Shugden

4 The benefits of relying upon Dorje Shugden

5 The way to rely upon Dorje Shugden

The previous incarnations of Dorje Shugden has seven parts:

1 Manjushri

2 Mahasiddha Biwawa

3 Sakya Pandita

4 Buton Rinchen Drub

5 Duldzin Dragpa Gyaltsen

6 Panchen Sonam Dragpa

7 Ngatrul Dragpa Gyaltsen

The way to rely upon Dorje Shugden has two parts:

1 The way to rely upon Dorje Shugden in thought and deed

2 The way to practise the sadhana of Dorje Shugden

Appendix II:

The Dharma Protector's Mandala

The Dharma Protector's Mandala

Part of Lama Losang Tubwang Dorjechang's Body	Corresponding Deity of the Body Mandala	Corresponding Deity of Dorje Shugden's Mandala
The five aggregates	*The five Buddha lineages*	*The five lineages of Dorje Shugden*
form	Vairochana	Vairochana Shugden
discrimination	Amitabha	Pema Shugden
consciousness	Akshobya	Dorje Shugden
feeling	Ratnasambhava	Ratna Shugden
compositional factors	Amoghasiddhi	Karma Shugden
The four elements	*The four Mothers*	*The nine Great Mothers*
earth	Lochana	Lochana
water	Mamaki	Mamaki
fire	Benzarahi	Benzarahi
wind	Tara	Tara
The five object sources	*The five Goddesses*	*The nine Great Mothers (cont.)*
forms	Rupavajra	Rupavajra
sounds	Shaptavajra	Shaptavajra
smells	Gändhavajra	Gändhavajra
tastes	Rasavajra	Rasavajra
tactile objects	Parshavajra	Parshavajra

Part of Lama Losang Tubwang Dorjechang's Body	Corresponding Deity of the Body Mandala	Corresponding Deity of Dorje Shugden's Mandala
The eight parts of the body	*The eight main Bodhisattvas*	*The eight Fully Ordained Monks*
eye sense power	Ksitigarbha	Ksitigarbha
ear sense power	Vajrapani	Vajrapani
nose sense power	Akashagarbha	Akashagarbha
tongue sense power	Avalokiteshvara	Avalokiteshvara
body sense power	Sarvanivarana-viskambini	Sarvanivarana-viskambini
mental power	Manjushri	Manjushri
veins	Maitreya	Maitreya
joints	Samantabhadra	Samantabhadra
The ten parts of the body	*The ten Wrathful Deities*	*The ten Wrathful Deities*
right hand	Yamantaka	Yamantaka
left hand	Aparajita	Aparajita
mouth	Hayagriva	Hayagriva
right shoulder	Achala	Achala
left shoulder	Takkiraja	Takkiraja
right knee	Niladanda	Niladanda
left knee	Mahabala	Mahabala
crown	Ushnishachakravarti	Ushnishachakravarti
soles of feet	Sumbharaja	Sumbharaja
secret place	Amritakundalini	Amritakundalini

Appendix III:

Sadhanas

CONTENTS

Liberating Prayer

PRAISE TO BUDDHA SHAKYAMUNI

O Blessed One, Shakyamuni Buddha,
Precious treasury of compassion,
Bestower of supreme inner peace,

You, who love all beings without exception,
Are the source of happiness and goodness;
And you guide us to the liberating path.

Your body is a wishfulfilling jewel,
Your speech is supreme, purifying nectar,
And your mind is refuge for all living
    beings.

With folded hands I turn to you,
Supreme unchanging friend,
I request from the depths of my heart:

Please give me the light of your wisdom
To dispel the darkness of my mind
And to heal my mental continuum.

Please nourish me with your goodness,
That I in turn may nourish all beings
With an unceasing banquet of delight.

Through your compassionate intention,
Your blessings and virtuous deeds,
And my strong wish to rely upon you.

May all suffering quickly cease
And all happiness and joy be fulfilled;
And may holy Dharma flourish for evermore.

Colophon: This prayer was composed by Venerable Geshe Kelsang Gyatso Rinpoche and is recited at the beginning of teachings, meditations and prayers in Kadampa Buddhist Centres throughout the world.

Heart Jewel

THE GURU YOGA OF JE TSONGKHAPA COMBINED
WITH THE CONDENSED SADHANA OF
HIS DHARMA PROTECTOR

Heart Jewel

Going for refuge

I and all sentient beings, until we achieve enlightenment,
Go for refuge to Buddha, Dharma and Sangha.

(3x)

Generating bodhichitta

Through the virtues I collect by giving and other
    perfections,
May I become a Buddha for the benefit of all.

(3x)

Inviting Je Tsongkhapa

From the heart of the Protector of the hundreds of Deities
    of the Joyful Land,
To the peak of a cloud which is like a cluster of fresh,
    white curd,
All-knowing Losang Dragpa, King of the Dharma,
Please come to this place together with your Sons.

Prayer of seven limbs

In the space before me on a lion throne, lotus and moon,
The venerable Gurus smile with delight.
O Supreme Field of Merit for my mind of faith,
Please remain for a hundred aeons to spread the doctrine.

Your mind of wisdom realizes the full extent of objects of
    knowledge,
Your eloquent speech is the ear-ornament of the fortunate,
Your beautiful body is ablaze with the glory of renown,
I prostrate to you, whom to see, to hear and to remember
    is so meaningful.

Pleasing water offerings, various flowers,
Sweet-smelling incense, lights, scented water and so forth,
A vast cloud of offerings both set out and imagined,
I offer to you, O Supreme Field of Merit.

Whatever non-virtues of body, speech and mind
I have accumulated since time without beginning,
Especially transgressions of my three vows,
With great remorse I confess each one from the depths of
    my heart.

In this degenerate age you strove for much learning and
    accomplishment.
Abandoning the eight worldly concerns, you made your
    freedom and endowment meaningful.
O Protector, from the very depths of my heart,
I rejoice in the great wave of your deeds.

From the billowing clouds of wisdom and compassion
In the space of your Truth Body, O Venerable and holy
    Gurus,
Please send down a rain of vast and profound Dharma
Appropriate to the disciples of this world.

Through the virtues I have accumulated here,
May the doctrine and all living beings receive every
    benefit.
Especially may the essence of the doctrine
Of Venerable Losang Dragpa shine forever.

Offering the mandala

The ground sprinkled with perfume and spread with
    flowers,
The Great Mountain, four lands, sun and moon,
Seen as a Buddha Land and offered thus,
May all beings enjoy such Pure Lands.

IDAM GURU RATNA MANDALAKAM NIRYATAYAMI

The *Migtsema* prayer

Tsongkhapa, crown ornament of the scholars of the Land
    of the Snows,
You are Avalokiteshvara, the treasury of unobservable
    compassion,
Manjushri, the supreme stainless wisdom,
And Vajrapani, the destroyer of the hosts of maras;
O Losang Dragpa I request you, please grant your
    blessings.   (7x, 21x, 100x, etc.)

Prayer of the stages of the path

The path begins with strong reliance
On my kind Teacher, source of all good;
O Bless me with this understanding
To follow him with great devotion.

This human life with all its freedoms,
Extremely rare, with so much meaning;
O Bless me with this understanding
All day and night to seize its essence.

My body, like a water bubble,
Decays and dies so very quickly;
After death come results of karma,
Just like the shadow of a body.

With this firm knowledge and remembrance
Bless me to be extremely cautious,
Always avoiding harmful actions
And gathering abundant virtue.

Samsara's pleasures are deceptive,
Give no contentment, only torment;
So please bless me to strive sincerely
To gain the bliss of perfect freedom.

O Bless me so that from this pure thought
Come mindfulness and greatest caution,
To keep as my essential practice
The doctrine's root, the Pratimoksha.

Just like myself all my kind mothers
Are drowning in samsara's ocean;
O So that I may soon release them,
Bless me to train in bodhichitta.

But I cannot become a Buddha
By this alone without three ethics;
So bless me with the strength to practise
The Bodhisattva's ordination.

By pacifying my distractions
And analyzing perfect meanings,
Bless me to quickly gain the union
Of special insight and quiescence.

When I become a pure container
Through common paths, bless me to enter
The essence practice of good fortune,
The supreme vehicle, Vajrayana.

The two attainments both depend on
My sacred vows and my commitments;
Bless me to understand this clearly
And keep them at the cost of my life.

By constant practice in four sessions,
The way explained by holy Teachers,
O Bless me to gain both the stages,
Which are the essence of the Tantras.

May those who guide me on the good path,
And my companions all have long lives;
Bless me to pacify completely
All obstacles, outer and inner.

May I always find perfect Teachers,
And take delight in holy Dharma,
Accomplish all grounds and paths swiftly,
And gain the state of Vajradhara.

Receiving blessings and purifying

From the hearts of all the holy beings, streams of light
and nectar flow down, granting blessings and purifying.

Requests to receive the Guru's blessings

O Glorious and precious root Guru,
Please sit on the lotus and moon seat at my heart.
Please care for me with your great kindness,
And grant me the blessings of your body, speech and
     mind.

O Glorious and precious root Guru,
Please sit on the lotus and moon seat at my heart.
Please care for me with your great kindness,
And bestow the common and supreme attainments.

O Glorious and precious root Guru,
Please sit on the lotus and moon seat at my heart.
Please care for me with your great kindness,
And remain firm until I attain the essence of
     enlightenment.

Dedication

Through being cared for throughout all my lives
By Conqueror Tsongkhapa as my Mahayana Guru,
May I never turn away, even for an instant,
From this excellent path praised by the Conquerors.

Inviting Dorje Shugden and his retinue

HUM
I have the clarity of the Yidam.
Before me in the centre of red and black fire and wind,
On a lotus and sun, trampling demons and obstructors,
Is a terrifying lion, which is powerful and alert.

Upon this sits the great king Dorje Shugden,
The supreme Heart Jewel of Dharma Protectors.
His body is clothed in the garments of a monk,
And on his head he wears a round, yellow hat.
His hands hold a sword and a heart of compassion.
To his followers he shows an expression of delight,
But to subdue demons and obstructors he displays a
    wrathful manner.
He is surrounded by a vast, assembled retinue,
Such as his attendant Khache Marpo and so forth.

Light rays from my heart instantly invite the wisdom
beings from the sphere of nature, and from all the
different palaces where they abide. They become
inseparable from the commitment beings.

Making offerings and requests

HUM
Respectfully I prostrate with body, speech and mind.
I offer a mass of inner and outer offerings, blissful
    tormas,
Alcohol, tea, cakes, milk and curd,
Both actually set out and mentally imagined, filling the
    whole of space.

Commitment, fulfilling, reliance and appropriate
    substances,
Outer, inner, secret, attractive and cleansing offerings,
    filling the whole of space,
I offer these to the entire assembly;
May I fulfil the heart commitment and restore my broken
    commitments.

All my harmful thoughts and actions
That have offended your mind, O Great Protector,
I confess from the depths of my heart.
Please purify them swiftly, and care for me with love,
   like a mother for her child.

I beseech you from the depths of my heart, O Supreme
   Deity,
Please cause the tradition of Je Tsongkhapa to flourish,
Extend the life and activities of the glorious Gurus,
And increase the study and practice of Dharma within
   the Dharma communities.

Please be with me always like the shadow of my body,
And grant me your unwavering care and protection.
Destroy all obstacles and adverse conditions,
Bestow favourable conditions, and fulfil all my wishes.

Now is the time to show clearly your versatile strength
Through your four actions, which are swift, incisive and
   unobstructed,
To fulfil quickly my special heartfelt desires
In accordance with my wishes;

Now is the time to distinguish the truth and falsity of
   actions and effects;
Now is the time to dispel false accusations against the
   innocent;
Now is the time to protect the pitiful and protectorless;
Now is the time to protect Dharma practitioners as your
   children.

In short, from now until I attain the essence of
enlightenment,
I shall honour you as the embodiment of my Guru, Deity
and Protector.
Therefore please watch over me during the three periods
of the day and the night
And never waver in your actions as my Protector.

Requesting the fulfilment of wishes

HUM
Whenever your followers with commitments
Request any of the four actions,
Swiftly, incisively, and without delay, you show signs for
all to see;
So please accomplish the actions that I now request of
you.

The stainless sun of Je Tsongkhapa's tradition
Shines throughout the sky of samsara and nirvana,
Eliminating the darkness of inferior and wrong paths;
Please cause its light to spread and bring good fortune to
all living beings.

May the glorious Gurus who uphold this tradition
Have indestructible lives, as stable as the supreme
victory banner;
May they send down a rain of deeds fulfilling the wishes
of disciples,
So that Je Tsongkhapa's doctrine will flourish.

Through increasing the study, practice, pure discipline
    and harmony
Of the communities who uphold the stainless doctrine of
    Buddha,
And who keep moral discipline with pure minds,
Please cause the Geden tradition to increase like a
    waxing moon.

Through your actions please fulfil the essential wishes
Of all practitioners who uphold the victory banner
Of practising single-pointedly the stages of the paths of
    Sutra and Tantra,
The essence of all the teachings they have heard.

Beings throughout this great earth are engaged in
    different actions
Of Dharma, non-Dharma, happiness, suffering, cause
    and effect;
Through your skilful deeds of preventing and nurturing,
Please lead all beings into the good path to ultimate
    happiness.

In particular, please destroy the obstacles and
    unfavourable conditions
Of myself and other practitioners.
Increase our lives, our merit and our resources,
And gather all things animate and inanimate to be freely
    enjoyed.

Please be with me always like the shadow of my body,
And care for me always like a friend,
By accomplishing swiftly whatever I wish for,
And whatever I ask of you.

Please perform immediately, without delaying for a year,
   or even for a month,
Appropriate actions to eliminate all obstacles
Caused by misguided beings with harmful minds who
   try to destroy Je Tsongkhapa's doctrine,
And especially by those who try to harm practitioners.

Please remain in this place always, surrounded by most
   excellent enjoyments.
As my guest, partake continuously of tormas and
   offerings;
And since you are entrusted with the protection of
   human wealth and enjoyments,
Never waver as my guardian throughout the day and the
   night.

All the attainments I desire
Arise from merely remembering you.
O Wishfulfilling Jewel, Protector of the Dharma,
Please accomplish all my wishes.   (3x)

Dedication

By this virtue may I quickly
Attain the enlightened state of the Guru,
And then lead every living being
Without exception to that ground.

Through my virtues from practising with pure
   motivation,
May all living beings, throughout all their lives,
Never be parted from peaceful and wrathful Manjushri,
But always come under their care.

Prayers for the Virtuous Tradition

So that the tradition of Je Tsongkhapa,
The King of the Dharma, may flourish,
May all obstacles be pacified
And may all favourable conditions abound.

Through the two collections of myself and others
Gathered throughout the three times,
May the doctrine of Conqueror Losang Dragpa
Flourish for evermore.

The nine-line *Migtsema* prayer

Tsongkhapa, crown ornament of the scholars of the Land
    of the Snows,
You are Buddha Shakyamuni and Vajradhara, the source
    of all attainments,
Avalokiteshvara, the treasury of unobservable
    compassion,
Manjushri, the supreme stainless wisdom,
And Vajrapani, the destroyer of the hosts of maras.
O Venerable Guru-Buddha, synthesis of all Three Jewels,
With my body, speech and mind, respectfully I make
    requests:
Please grant your blessings to ripen and liberate myself
    and others,
And bestow the common and supreme attainments.

(3x)

Colophon: This sadhana or ritual prayer for spiritual
attainments was compiled from traditional sources by Venerable
Geshe Kelsang Gyatso Rinpoche, and translated under his
compassionate guidance.

King of the Dharma

A METHOD FOR ACCOMPLISHING
SELF-GENERATION AS JE TSONGKHAPA

King of the Dharma

Going for refuge

I and all sentient beings, until we achieve enlightenment,
Go for refuge to Buddha, Dharma and Sangha.

(3x)

Generating bodhichitta

Through the virtues I collect by giving and other
    perfections,
May I become a Buddha for the benefit of all.

(3x)

Inviting Je Tsongkhapa

From the heart of the Protector of the hundreds of Deities
    of the Joyful Land,
To the peak of a cloud which is like a cluster of fresh,
    white curd,
All-knowing Losang Dragpa, King of the Dharma,
Please come to this place together with your Sons.

Prayer of seven limbs

In the space before me on a lion throne, lotus and moon,
The venerable Gurus smile with delight.
O Supreme Field of Merit for my mind of faith,
Please remain for a hundred aeons to spread the
    doctrine.

Your mind of wisdom realizes the full extent of objects of
    knowledge,
Your eloquent speech is the ear-ornament of the
    fortunate,
Your beautiful body is ablaze with the glory of renown,
I prostrate to you, whom to see, to hear and to remember
    is so meaningful.

Pleasing water offerings, various flowers,
Sweet-smelling incense, lights, scented water, and so
    forth,
A vast cloud of offerings both set out and imagined,
I offer to you, O Supreme Field of Merit.

Whatever non-virtues of body, speech and mind
I have accumulated since time without beginning,
Especially transgressions of my three vows,
With great remorse I confess each one from the depths of
    my heart.

In this degenerate age you strove for much learning and
    accomplishment.
Abandoning the eight worldly concerns, you made your
    freedom and endowment meaningful.
O Protector, from the very depths of my heart,
I rejoice in the great wave of your deeds.

From the billowing clouds of wisdom and compassion
In the space of your Truth Body, O Venerable and holy
    Gurus,
Please send down a rain of vast and profound Dharma
Appropriate to the disciples of this world.

Through the virtues I have accumulated here,
May the doctrine and all living beings receive every
    benefit.
Especially may the essence of the doctrine
Of Venerable Losang Dragpa shine forever.

Offering the mandala

The ground sprinkled with perfume and spread with
    flowers,
The Great Mountain, four lands, sun and moon,
Seen as a Buddha Land and offered thus,
May all beings enjoy such Pure Lands.

IDAM GURU RATNA MANDALAKAM NIRYATAYAMI

The *Migtsema* prayer

Tsongkhapa, crown ornament of the scholars of the Land
    of the Snows,
You are Avalokiteshvara, the treasury of unobservable
    compassion,
Manjushri, the supreme stainless wisdom,
And Vajrapani, the destroyer of the hosts of maras;
O Losang Dragpa I request you, please grant your
    blessings.   (7x, 21x, 100x, etc.)

The letter DHI

Requests to receive the Guru's blessings

O Glorious and precious root Guru,
Please sit on the lotus and moon seat at my heart.
Please care for me with your great kindness,
And grant me the blessings of your body, speech and mind.

O Glorious and precious root Guru,
Please sit on the lotus and moon seat at my heart.
Please care for me with your great kindness,
And bestow the common and supreme attainments.

O Glorious and precious root Guru,
Please sit on the lotus and moon seat at my heart.
Please care for me with your great kindness,
And remain firm until I attain the essence of enlightenment.

Self-generation as Je Tsongkhapa

OM SÖBHAWA SHUDDHA SARWA DHARMA SÖBHAWA
    SHUDDHO HAM
OM SHUNYATA GYANA VAJRA SÖBHAWA ÄMAKO HAM
Everything becomes emptiness.

From the state of emptiness, in my place, there appears
a jewelled throne supported by eight great lions. Upon
this from PAM comes a lotus and from AH comes a moon.
Upon this my mind appears as an orange letter DHI,
which transforms into a sword marked by a letter DHI.

From this, light rays radiate, making offerings to the
Superior beings and fulfilling the welfare of sentient
beings. Gathering back, they completely transform and I
arise as the great Tsongkhapa, the King of the Dharma of
the three realms and the essence of all the Conquerors. I
have a completely pure body, speech and mind.

I have a white-coloured body, one face, and two hands. My body is clothed in the three saffron robes of an ordained person, and on my head I wear a golden long-eared Pandit's hat. My hands, at the level of my heart in the gesture of turning the Wheel of Dharma, hold between the thumbs and forefingers the stems of upala flowers, which blossom at the level of my right and left ears. On the right flower is a wisdom sword and on the left is a scripture of the *Perfection of Wisdom Sutra in Eight Thousand Lines*.

My body is adorned with the signs and indications of a Buddha, and is clear and translucent, the nature of light. I sit with my legs crossed in the vajra posture in the centre of a mass of light that radiates from my body.

At the centre of my crown chakra, on a lotus and moon cushion, is Manjushri, who is orange in colour with one face and two arms. At the centre of my throat chakra, on a lotus and moon cushion, is Avalokiteshvara, who is white in colour with one face and four arms. At the centre of my heart chakra, on a lotus and sun cushion, is Vajrapani, who is blue in colour with one face and two arms. They are complete with their usual features, such as ornaments, clothes, gestures and implements.

At the heart of Manjushri is a white letter OM, at the heart of Avalokiteshvara is a red letter AH, and at the heart of Vajrapani is a blue letter HUM.

From the HUM at my heart, light rays radiate inviting the great Tsongkhapa, the King of the Dharma, to come from Tushita Pure Land.

DZA HUM BAM HO
We become non-dual.

Blessing the offerings to the self-generated Deity

OM VAJRA AMRITA KUNDALI HANA HANA PHAT
OM SÖBHAWA SHUDDHA SARWA SHARMA SÖBHAWA
    SHUDDHI HAM
Everything becomes emptiness.

From the state of emptiness, from DHRUM letters come
broad and expansive jewelled vessels. Inside each of
these there is a letter OM, which melts into light and
there arise heavenly offering substances.

OM AHRGHAM AH HUM
OM PADÄM AH HUM
OM PUPE AH HUM
OM DHUPE AH HUM
OM ALOKE AH HUM
OM GÄNDHE AH HUM
OM NEWIDE AH HUM
OM SHAPTA AH HUM

Making offerings to the self-generated Deity

OM GURU SUMATI KIRTI AHRGHAM PARTITZA HUM
    SÖHA
OM GURU SUMATI KIRTI PADÄM PARTITZA HUM SÖHA
OM GURU SUMATI KIRTI PUPE PARTITZA HUM SÖHA
OM GURU SUMATI KIRTI DHUPE PARTITZA HUM SÖHA
OM GURU SUMATI KIRTI ALOKE PARTITZA HUM SÖHA
OM GURU SUMATI KIRTI GÄNDHE PARTITZA HUM SÖHA
OM GURU SUMATI KIRTI NEWIDE PARTITZA HUM SÖHA
OM GURU SUMATI KIRTI SHAPTA PARTITZA HUM SÖHA

Praise to the self-generated Deity

I prostrate to you, O Glorious and venerable precious
    Guru,
Who are kinder than all the Buddhas,
The sole eyes of migrating beings of the three realms,
And the Protector of all those who seek liberation.

Meditating on divine pride and clear appearance

*At this point we meditate on divine pride and clear
appearance according to the commentary.*

Reciting the mantras

On a moon cushion at the heart of Manjushri abiding at
the centre of my crown chakra is a letter DHI encircled
clockwise by the orange letters OM AH RA PA TSA NA.
On a moon cushion at the heart of Avalokiteshvara
abiding at the centre of my throat chakra is a letter HRIH
encircled clockwise by the white letters OM MANI PÄME
HUM. On a sun cushion at the heart of Vajrapani abiding
at the centre of my heart chakra is a letter HUM encircled
clockwise by the blue letters OM AH VAJRAPANI HUM
HUM PHAT

From the letter DHI and the mantra at Manjushri's
heart, infinite rays of light radiate and touch the body
and mind of all sentient beings. The light purifies the
inner darkness of their ignorance and they attain divine
wisdom eyes.

OM AH RA PA TSA NA DHI   (100x)

From the letter HRIH and the mantra at Avalokiteshvara's heart, infinite rays of light radiate and touch the body and mind of all sentient beings of the six realms. The light purifies all their negative karma and they experience uncontaminated happiness.

OM MANI PÄME HUM   (100x)

From the letter HUM and the mantra at Vajrapani's heart, infinite rays of light radiate and touch the body and mind of all sentient beings. The light pacifies all their obstacles to gaining liberation and full enlightenment, and they all conquer the four maras and attain Buddhahood.

OM AH VAJRAPANI HUM HUM PHAT   (100x)

Manjushri dissolves into my body, whereby my body becomes the nature of Manjushri; Avalokiteshvara dissolves into my speech, whereby my speech becomes the nature of Avalokiteshvara; and Vajrapani dissolves into my mind, whereby my mind becomes the nature of Vajrapani.

Actual recitation of the *Migtsema* mantra

On a moon cushion at my heart, my mind appears in the aspect of an orange letter DHI encircled clockwise by the *Migtsema* mantra. From the mantra and letter DHI, infinite rays of light radiate to the ten directions, drawing back the blessings of the body, speech and mind of all the Buddhas in the aspect of white, red and blue rays of light. These dissolve into my mind, the letter DHI at my heart, and I receive the blessings of the body, speech and mind of all the Buddhas.

Tsongkhapa, crown ornament of the scholars of the Land
of the Snows,
You are Avalokiteshvara, the treasury of unobservable
compassion,
Manjushri, the supreme stainless wisdom,
And Vajrapani, the destroyer of the hosts of maras;
O Losang Dragpa I request you, please grant your
blessings.

Recite as many times as you wish.

Blessing the offerings to the in-front-generation

OM VAJRA AMRITA KUNDALI HANA HANA PHAT
OM SÖBHAWA SHUDDHA SARWA SHARMA SÖBHAWA
SHUDDHI HAM
Everything becomes emptiness.

From the state of emptiness, from DHRUM letters come
broad and expansive jewelled vessels. Inside each of
these there is a letter OM, which melts into light and
there arise heavenly offering substances.

OM AHRGHAM AH HUM
OM PADÄM AH HUM
OM PUPE AH HUM
OM DHUPE AH HUM
OM ALOKE AH HUM
OM GÄNDHE AH HUM
OM NEWIDE AH HUM
OM SHAPTA AH HUM

Blessing the torma

OM VAJRA AMRITA KUNDALI HANA HANA PHAT
OM SÖBHAWA SHUDDHA SARWA SHARMA SÖBHAWA
    SHUDDHI HAM
Everything becomes emptiness.

From the state of emptiness, from a DHRUM before
me comes a broad and expansive jewelled vessel.
Inside from a letter OM comes a torma, a vast ocean of
uncontaminated nectar of exalted wisdom, which is
brilliant and pervasive.
OM AH HUM   (3x)

Inviting the guests of the torma offering

From the letter DHI at my heart, light rays radiate and
invite the King of the Dharma, the great Tsongkhapa,
surrounded by the assembly of Buddhas and
Bodhisattvas, to come to the space before me. They
partake of the essence of the torma by drawing it through
their tongues, which are straws of vajra light.

Actual torma offering

OM GURU SUMATI KIRTI SAPARIWARA IDAM BALINGTA
KHA KHA KHAHI KHAHI   (3x)

Making offerings

OM GURU SUMATI KIRTI AHRGHAM PARTITZA HUM
    SÖHA
OM GURU SUMATI KIRTI PADÄM PARTITZA HUM SÖHA
OM GURU SUMATI KIRTI PUPE PARTITZA HUM SÖHA

OM GURU SUMATI KIRTI DHUPE PARTITZA HUM SÖHA
OM GURU SUMATI KIRTI ALOKE PARTITZA HUM SÖHA
OM GURU SUMATI KIRTI GÄNDHE PARTITZA HUM SÖHA
OM GURU SUMATI KIRTI NEWIDE PARTITZA HUM SÖHA
OM GURU SUMATI KIRTI SHAPTA PARTITZA HUM SÖHA

Praise

I prostrate to you, O Glorious and venerable precious
    Guru,
Who are kinder than all the Buddhas,
The sole eyes of migrating beings of the three realms,
And the Protector of all those who seek liberation.

Requesting forbearance

OM VAJRA SATTÖ AH   (3x)

Whatever mistakes I have made
Through not finding, not understanding,
Or not having the ability,
Please, O Protector, be patient with all of these.

Dissolving Guru Tsongkhapa into our heart

The holy beings, guests of the torma offering, dissolve
into Guru Tsongkhapa, and he dissolves into my mind,
which is in the aspect of Je Tsongkhapa at my heart.

Dedication

Thus, through my virtues from making offerings and
    requests
To the Venerable Guru, the source of all attainments,
May I always come under the special care
Of Guru Manjushri throughout all my lives.

Through meditating on Buddha Maitreya
And the precious Tushita Pure Land,
May I accomplish that Pure Land and take rebirth there
Immediately after this life.

Through inviting the Venerable Guru and his two Sons
From Maitreya's heart to the peak of a cloud,
And accumulating merit through the seven limbs,
May I easily ripen all my virtuous seeds.

Through my practice of the *Migtsema* prayer
With the strong recognition of Guru Tsongkhapa
As the embodiment of the three holy beings,
May all living beings attain the holy state of a Buddha.

Auspicious prayer

When I meet the holy Dharma of Je Tsongkhapa
And practise sincerely by means of the ten Dharma
    actions,
May all the powerful Dharma Protectors assist me,
And may a great ocean of auspiciousness pervade all
    directions.

Prayers for the Virtuous Tradition

So that the tradition of Je Tsongkhapa,
The King of the Dharma, may flourish,
May all obstacles be pacified
And may all favourable conditions abound.

Through the two collections of myself and others
Gathered throughout the three times,
May the doctrine of Conqueror Losang Dragpa
Flourish for evermore.

The nine-line *Migtsema* prayer

Tsongkhapa, crown ornament of the scholars of the Land
    of the Snows,
You are Buddha Shakyamuni and Vajradhara, the source
    of all attainments,
Avalokiteshvara, the treasury of unobservable compassion,
Manjushri, the supreme stainless wisdom,
And Vajrapani, the destroyer of the hosts of maras.
O Venerable Guru-Buddha, synthesis of all Three Jewels,
With my body, speech and mind, respectfully I make
    requests:
Please grant your blessings to ripen and liberate myself
    and others,
And bestow the common and supreme attainments.

(3x)

Colophon: This sadhana or ritual prayer for
spiritual attainments was composed by
Venerable Geshe Kelsang Gyatso Rinpoche.

Wishfulfilling Jewel

THE GURU YOGA OF JE TSONGKHAPA
COMBINED WITH THE SADHANA OF
HIS DHARMA PROTECTOR

Wishfulfilling Jewel

Going for refuge

I and all sentient beings, until we achieve enlightenment,
Go for refuge to Buddha, Dharma and Sangha.

(3x)

Generating bodhichitta

Through the virtues I collect by giving and other
    perfections,
May I become a Buddha for the benefit of all.

(3x)

Inviting Je Tsongkhapa

From the heart of the Protector of the hundreds of
    Deities of the Joyful Land,
To the peak of a cloud which is like a cluster of fresh,
    white curd,
All-knowing Losang Dragpa, King of the Dharma,
Please come to this place together with your Sons.

Prayer of seven limbs

In the space before me on a lion throne, lotus and moon,
The venerable Gurus smile with delight.
O Supreme Field of Merit for my mind of faith,
Please remain for a hundred aeons to spread the doctrine.

Your mind of wisdom realizes the full extent of objects of
    knowledge,
Your eloquent speech is the ear-ornament of the fortunate,
Your beautiful body is ablaze with the glory of renown,
I prostrate to you, whom to see, to hear and to remember
    is so meaningful.

Pleasing water offerings, various flowers,
Sweet-smelling incense, lights, scented water and so forth,
A vast cloud of offerings both set out and imagined,
I offer to you, O Supreme Field of Merit.

Whatever non-virtues of body, speech and mind
I have accumulated since time without beginning,
Especially transgressions of my three vows,
With great remorse I confess each one from the depths of
    my heart.

In this degenerate age you strove for much learning and
    accomplishment.
Abandoning the eight worldly concerns, you made your
    freedom and endowment meaningful.
O Protector, from the very depths of my heart,
I rejoice in the great wave of your deeds.

From the billowing clouds of wisdom and compassion
In the space of your Truth Body, O Venerable and holy
Gurus,
Please send down a rain of vast and profound Dharma
Appropriate to the disciples of this world.

Through the virtues I have accumulated here,
May the doctrine and all living beings receive every
benefit.
Especially may the essence of the doctrine
Of Venerable Losang Dragpa shine forever.

Offering the mandala

The ground sprinkled with perfume and spread with
flowers,
The Great Mountain, four lands, sun and moon,
Seen as a Buddha Land and offered thus,
May all beings enjoy such Pure Lands.

IDAM GURU RATNA MANDALAKAM NIRYATAYAMI

The *Migtsema* prayer

Tsongkhapa, crown ornament of the scholars of the Land
of the Snows,
You are Avalokiteshvara, the treasury of unobservable
compassion,
Manjushri, the supreme stainless wisdom,
And Vajrapani, the destroyer of the hosts of maras;
O Losang Dragpa I request you, please grant your
blessings.   (7x, 21x, 100x, etc.)

174

Prayer of the stages of the path

The path begins with strong reliance
On my kind Teacher, source of all good;
O Bless me with this understanding
To follow him with great devotion.

This human life with all its freedoms,
Extremely rare, with so much meaning;
O Bless me with this understanding
All day and night to seize its essence.

My body, like a water bubble,
Decays and dies so very quickly;
After death come results of karma,
Just like the shadow of a body.

With this firm knowledge and remembrance
Bless me to be extremely cautious,
Always avoiding harmful actions
And gathering abundant virtue.

Samsara's pleasures are deceptive,
Give no contentment, only torment;
So please bless me to strive sincerely
To gain the bliss of perfect freedom.

O Bless me so that from this pure thought
Come mindfulness and greatest caution,
To keep as my essential practice
The doctrine's root, the Pratimoksha.

Just like myself all my kind mothers
Are drowning in samsara's ocean;
O So that I may soon release them,
Bless me to train in bodhichitta.

But I cannot become a Buddha
By this alone without three ethics;
So bless me with the strength to practise
The Bodhisattva's ordination.

By pacifying my distractions
And analyzing perfect meanings,
Bless me to quickly gain the union
Of special insight and quiescence.

When I become a pure container
Through common paths, bless me to enter
The essence practice of good fortune,
The supreme vehicle, Vajrayana.

The two attainments both depend on
My sacred vows and my commitments;
Bless me to understand this clearly
And keep them at the cost of my life.

By constant practice in four sessions,
The way explained by holy Teachers,
O Bless me to gain both the stages,
Which are the essence of the Tantras.

May those who guide me on the good path,
And my companions all have long lives;
Bless me to pacify completely
All obstacles, outer and inner.

May I always find perfect Teachers,
And take delight in holy Dharma,
Accomplish all grounds and paths swiftly,
And gain the state of Vajradhara.

Receiving blessings and purifying

From the hearts of all the holy beings, streams of light
and nectar flow down, granting blessings and purifying.

Requests to receive the Guru's blessings

O Glorious and precious root Guru,
Please sit on the lotus and moon seat at my heart.
Please care for me with your great kindness,
And grant me the blessings of your body, speech and
    mind.

O Glorious and precious root Guru,
Please sit on the lotus and moon seat at my heart.
Please care for me with your great kindness,
And bestow the common and supreme attainments.

O Glorious and precious root Guru,
Please sit on the lotus and moon seat at my heart.
Please care for me with your great kindness,
And remain firm until I attain the essence of
    enlightenment.

Dedication

Through being cared for throughout all my lives
By Conqueror Tsongkhapa as my Mahayana Guru,
May I never turn away, even for an instant,
From this excellent path praised by the Conquerors.

Inviting Dorje Shugden and his retinue

HUM

I have the clarity of the Yidam.

Before me in the centre of red and black fire and wind,

On a lotus and sun, trampling demons and obstructors,

Is a terrifying lion, which is powerful and alert.

Upon this sits the great king Dorje Shugden,

The supreme Heart Jewel of Dharma Protectors.

His body is clothed in the garments of a monk,

And on his head he wears a round, yellow hat.

His hands hold a sword and a heart of compassion.

To his followers he shows an expression of delight,

But to subdue demons and obstructors he displays a
wrathful manner.

He is surrounded by a vast, assembled retinue,

Such as his attendant Khache Marpo and so forth.

Light rays from my heart instantly invite the wisdom
beings from the sphere of nature, and from all the
different palaces where they abide. They become
inseparable from the commitment beings.

Making offerings and requests

HUM

Respectfully I prostrate with body, speech and mind.

I offer a mass of inner and outer offerings, blissful
tormas,

Alcohol, tea, cakes, milk and curd,

Both actually set out and mentally imagined, filling the
whole of space.

Commitment, fulfilling, reliance and appropriate
    substances,
Outer, inner, secret, attractive and cleansing offerings,
    filling the whole of space,
I offer these to the entire assembly;
May I fulfil the heart commitment and restore my broken
    commitments.

All my harmful thoughts and actions
That have offended your mind, O Great Protector,
I confess from the depths of my heart.
Please purify them swiftly, and care for me with love,
    like a mother for her child.

I beseech you from the depths of my heart, O Supreme
    Deity,
Please cause the tradition of Je Tsongkhapa to flourish,
Extend the life and activities of the glorious Gurus,
And increase the study and practice of Dharma within
    the Dharma communities.

Please be with me always like the shadow of my body,
And grant me your unwavering care and protection.
Destroy all obstacles and adverse conditions,
Bestow favourable conditions, and fulfil all my wishes.

Now is the time to show clearly your versatile strength
Through your four actions, which are swift, incisive and
    unobstructed,
To fulfil quickly my special heartfelt desires
In accordance with my wishes;

Now is the time to distinguish the truth and falsity of
actions and effects;
Now is the time to dispel false accusations against the
innocent;
Now is the time to protect the pitiful and protectorless;
Now is the time to protect Dharma practitioners as your
children.

In short, from now until I attain the essence of
enlightenment,
I shall honour you as the embodiment of my Guru, Deity
and Protector.
Therefore please watch over me during the three periods
of the day and the night
And never waver in your actions as my Protector.

Recitation of the mantra

I have the clarity of the Yidam. Before me are the five
lineages of Dorje Shugden, the great king of Dharma
Protectors. At their hearts are sun cushions, upon each
of which there is a HUM surrounded by the mantra
rosary in its appropriate colour. Light rays radiate from
the seed-letter at my heart and touch these. As a result
their minds automatically engage in the pacifying,
increasing, controlling and wrathful actions that I desire,
accomplishing them without obstruction.

OM VAJRA WIKI WITRANA SÖHA   (21x, 100x, etc.)

OM DHARMAPALA MAHA RADZA VAJRA BEGAWÄN
RUDRA: PÄNTSA KULA SARWA SHA TRUM MARAYA
HUM PHAT   (7x, 21x, etc.)

Blessing the tormas

OM KHANDAROHI HUM HUM PHAT
OM SÖBHAWA SHUDDHA SARWA DHARMA SÖBHAWA
    SHUDDHO HAM
Everything becomes emptiness.

From the state of emptiness, from YAM comes wind, from
RAM comes fire, from AH a grate of three human heads.
Upon this, from AH appears a broad and expansive
skullcup, inside which are the five meats and the five
nectars. These are purified, transformed, and increased
by the three letters, and become a great ocean of
uncontaminated nectar of exalted wisdom.
OM AH HUM   (3x)

Visualizing the guests of the tormas

Before me are the five lineages of Dorje Shugden, the
great king of Dharma Protectors, together with their
retinues. From HUMs in their tongues come red, single-
pronged vajras. These have straws of light through
which they partake of all the essence of the tormas.

Offering the tormas to the five lineages

OM DHARMAPALA MAHA RADZA VAJRA BEGAWÄN
RUDRA: PÄNTSA KULA SAPARIWARA SARWA BIGNÄN
SHA TRUM IDAM BALINGTA KHA KHA KHAHI
KHAHI   (3x)

Offering the tormas to the retinues

OM AHKAROMUKHAM SARWA DHARMANÄN
ADENUWATEN NADÖ DA, NAMA SARWA TATHAGATA
AWALOKITE OM SAMBHARA SAMBHARA HUM   (3x)

Outer offerings

OM DHARMAPALA MAHA RADZA VAJRA BEGAWÄN
RUDRA: PÄNTSA KULA SAPARIWARA AHRGHAM,
PADÄM, PUPE, DHUPE, ALOKE, GÄNDHE, NEWIDE,
SHAPTA PARTITZA HUM SÖHA

Inner offering

OM DHARMAPALA MAHA RADZA VAJRA BEGAWÄN
RUDRA: PÄNTSA KULA SAPARIWARA OM AH HUM

Special request to Dorje Shugden

HUM
O Five lineages of Dorje Shugden together with your
retinues, Protectors of the doctrine of Je Tsongkhapa,
please accept these blissful tormas. Please protect
the doctrine of Buddha, and especially the Sutra and
Tantra teachings of the Protector Manjushri, King of
the Dharma, the great Tsongkhapa. Please increase the
renown of the Three Jewels, protect the community of
the Sangha, and extend the life of the Gurus. For myself,
the practitioner, and all of us disciples, our benefactors,
and others, please dispel all adverse conditions that
obstruct the practice of Dharma. Please establish
favourable conditions and subdue immediately all
traitors, enemies, and obstructors who cause harm and
injury, by performing the appropriate actions swiftly and
without delay!

OM DHARMAPALA MAHA RADZA VAJRA BEGAWÄN
RUDRA: PÄNTSA KULA SAPARIWARA DRA GEG AH MU
KA MARAYA PHAT!

Blessing the tsog offering

OM KHANDAROHI HUM HUM PHAT
OM SÖBHAWA SHUDDHA SARWA DHARMA SÖBHAWA
    SHUDDHO HAM
Everything becomes emptiness.

From the state of emptiness, from YAM comes wind, from
RAM comes fire, from AH a grate of three human heads.
Upon this, from AH appears a broad and expansive
skullcup, inside which are the five meats and the five
nectars. These are purified, transformed, and increased
by the three letters, and become a great ocean of
uncontaminated nectar of exalted wisdom.
OM AH HUM   (3x)

Short tsog offering

HUM
I make this tsog offering of uncontaminated enjoyments
To the assembly of Gurus, Yidams, Three Jewels,
    Dakinis, and oath-bound Protectors;
And especially to you, great king Dorje Shugden,
Supreme Protector of the doctrine of the Geden tradition,
And to the whole assembly who follow your command.
By your accepting this, may the Conqueror Losang's
    tradition
Spread throughout the ten directions.
For all of us disciples, our benefactors, and others,
Please destroy all outer, inner and secret obstacles.
Please subdue hateful enemies and harmful obstructors,
And swiftly fulfil all our wishes.   (3x)

Tsog offering to the Guru

HO

O Great Hero please listen to me.
Of this we should have no doubt,
Brahmins, dogs, and outcasts are inseparably one.
Considering this, please enjoy this offering.

HO

I am the principal of all the Conquerors,
In actuality the Blessed One Guru Heruka.
I taste this great ocean of wisdom nectar
To satisfy all the Deities.

AH HO MAHA SUKHA

Blessing the golden drink (serkyem)

OM KHANDAROHI HUM HUM PHAT
OM SÖBHAWA SHUDDHA SARWA DHARMA SÖBHAWA
SHUDDHO HAM
Everything becomes emptiness.

From the state of emptiness, from AH appears a broad
and expansive skullcup. Inside this is the golden drink,
which is the nature of the five meats and the five nectars.
This is purified, transformed, and increased by the three
letters, and becomes a great ocean of uncontaminated
nectar of exalted wisdom.

OM AH HUM   (3x)

Offering the golden drink (serkyem)

HUM

To the Gurus who perform the two purposes and send
    down a rain of excellent blessings,

And to the Yidams who bestow all common and
    uncommon attainments,

I offer this drink of nectar that bestows bliss;

Please partake, and swiftly and spontaneously fulfil all
    my wishes.

To the whole assembly of Heroes and Dakinis of the
    three places,

And to the assembly of powerful, oath-bound Dharma
    Protectors,

I offer this drink of nectar that bestows bliss;

Please partake, and swiftly and spontaneously fulfil all
    my wishes.

Especially to you, supreme, supramundane Protector of
    the doctrine,

Very powerful, swift, and wrathful Dorje Shugden,

I offer this drink of nectar that bestows bliss;

Please partake, and swiftly and spontaneously fulfil all
    my wishes.

To you, manifestations of the five lineages, who bestow
    without obstruction

Countless pacifying, increasing, controlling and
    wrathful actions,

I offer this drink of nectar that bestows bliss;

Please partake, and swiftly and spontaneously fulfil all
    my wishes.

To the nine attractive Mothers, the eight guiding Monks,
The ten youthful and wrathful Assistants, and so forth,
I offer this drink of nectar that bestows bliss;
Please partake, and swiftly and spontaneously fulfil all
    my wishes.

To the extremely wrathful Khache Marpo,
The fierce Attendant who opposes those who betray the
    Dharma,
I offer this drink of nectar that bestows bliss;
Please partake, and swiftly and spontaneously fulfil all
    my wishes.

And to all your emanations and their emanations in turn
    who are beyond thought,
The Attendants, gods, and others filling the three
    thousand worlds,
I offer this drink of nectar that bestows bliss;
Please partake, and swiftly and spontaneously fulfil all
    my wishes.

Thus, through the power of my making offerings and
    requesting your help,
Please perform the four types of action during the six times;
And always care for me and protect me like a father with
    his child,
Without wavering even for a moment.

And may you, the whole assembly of dignified Attendants,
Ever mindful of your solemn oaths to Venerable Duldzin,
Accomplish swiftly and without wavering
Whatever actions I may request of you.

Requesting the fulfilment of wishes

HUM
Whenever your followers with commitments
Request any of the four actions,
Swiftly, incisively, and without delay, you show signs for
all to see;
So please accomplish the actions that I now request of you.

The stainless sun of Je Tsongkhapa's tradition
Shines throughout the sky of samsara and nirvana,
Eliminating the darkness of inferior and wrong paths;
Please cause its light to spread and bring good fortune to
all living beings.

May the glorious Gurus who uphold this tradition
Have indestructible lives, as stable as the supreme
victory banner;
May they send down a rain of deeds fulfilling the wishes
of disciples,
So that Je Tsongkhapa's doctrine will flourish.

Through increasing the study, practice, pure discipline,
and harmony
Of the communities who uphold the stainless doctrine of
Buddha,
And who keep moral discipline with pure minds,
Please cause the Geden tradition to increase like a
waxing moon.

Through your actions please fulfil the essential wishes
Of all practitioners who uphold the victory banner
Of practising single-pointedly the stages of the paths of
Sutra and Tantra,
The essence of all the teachings they have heard.

Beings throughout this great earth are engaged in different
   actions
Of Dharma, non-Dharma, happiness, suffering, cause and
   effect;
Through your skilful deeds of preventing and nurturing,
Please lead all beings into the good path to ultimate happiness.

In particular, please destroy the obstacles and
   unfavourable conditions
Of myself and other practitioners.
Increase our lives, our merit, and our resources,
And gather all things animate and inanimate to be freely
   enjoyed.

Please be with me always like the shadow of my body,
And care for me always like a friend,
By accomplishing swiftly whatever I wish for,
And whatever I ask of you.

Please perform immediately, without delaying for a year,
   or even for a month,
Appropriate actions to eliminate all obstacles
Caused by misguided beings with harmful minds who try
   to destroy Je Tsongkhapa's doctrine,
And especially by those who try to harm practitioners.

Please remain in this place always, surrounded by most
   excellent enjoyments.
As my guest, partake continuously of tormas and
   offerings;
And since you are entrusted with the protection of human
   wealth and enjoyments,
Never waver as my guardian throughout the day and the
   night.

All the attainments I desire
Arise from merely remembering you.
O Wishfulfilling Jewel, Protector of the Dharma,
Please accomplish all my wishes.　　　(3x)

Giving the remaining tsog offering to the spirits

OM AH HUM　　　(3x)

HUM
I make this tsog offering of uncontaminated nectar
To the assembly of guests, the regional guardians.
May you enjoy it with delight,
And assist practitioners with your actions.

Dedication

By this virtue may I quickly
Attain the enlightened state of the Guru,
And then lead every living being
Without exception to that ground.

Through my virtues from practising with pure motivation,
May all living beings, throughout all their lives,
Never be parted from peaceful and wrathful Manjushri,
But always come under their care.

Auspicious prayer

May there be the auspiciousness of the root and lineage
　　　Gurus,
May there be the auspiciousness of the assembly of Deities
　　　and Yidams,
May there be the auspiciousness of the Dakas and Dakinis,
And may there be the auspiciousness of the Dharma
　　　Protectors.

Prayers for the Virtuous Tradition

So that the tradition of Je Tsongkhapa,
The King of the Dharma, may flourish,
May all obstacles be pacified
And may all favourable conditions abound.

Through the two collections of myself and others
Gathered throughout the three times,
May the doctrine of Conqueror Losang Dragpa
Flourish for evermore.

The nine-line *Migtsema* prayer

Tsongkhapa, crown ornament of the scholars of the Land
    of the Snows,
You are Buddha Shakyamuni and Vajradhara, the source
    of all attainments,
Avalokiteshvara, the treasury of unobservable
    compassion,
Manjushri, the supreme stainless wisdom,
And Vajrapani, the destroyer of the hosts of maras.
O Venerable Guru-Buddha, synthesis of all Three Jewels,
With my body, speech and mind, respectfully I make
    requests:
Please grant your blessings to ripen and liberate myself
    and others,
And bestow the common and supreme attainments.

(3x)

Colophon: This sadhana or ritual prayer for spiritual
attainments was compiled from traditional sources by
Venerable Geshe Kelsang Gyatso Rinpoche, and translated
under his compassionate guidance.

Vajradaka Burning Offering

A PRACTICE FOR PURIFYING
MISTAKES AND NEGATIVITIES

by
Ngulchu Dharmabhadra

Vajradaka Burning Offering

Going for refuge

I and all sentient beings, until we achieve enlightenment,
Go for refuge to Buddha, Dharma and Sangha.   (3x)

Generating bodhichitta

Through the virtues I collect by giving and other perfections,
May I become a Buddha for the benefit of all.   (3x)

Generating special bodhichitta

And especially for the sake of all mother sentient beings,
I must attain the state of complete Buddhahood as quickly
as possible. Therefore I shall engage in a burning offering
to Vajradaka.

Visualizing the commitment being

OM VAJRA AMRITA KUNDALI HANA HANA HUM PHAT
OM SÖBHAWA SHUDDHA SARWA DHARMA SÖBHAWA
    SHUDDHO HAM
The fire becomes emptiness.

From the state of emptiness, there arises a fiercely blazing
fire of exalted wisdom. In the centre of this, from a HUM
and a vajra, there arises wrathful Vajradaka, dark blue in

colour. He has one face and two hands, which are joined
in the mudra of a Hungdze and hold a vajra and bell. With
his mouth wide open, he snarls into space, baring his four
sharp fangs. His head is adorned with five dry skulls and
he wears a long necklace of fifty moist skulls. He wears a
tiger's skin for a lower garment and is complete with all
the features of a wrathful manifestation. He sits with his
legs forming a circle, in the manner of a Hero destroying
negativities and obstructions. At his crown is a white OM,
at his throat a red AH, at his heart a blue HUM.

Inviting and absorbing the wisdom beings

Light rays radiate from the HUM at his heart and invite
from their natural abodes wisdom beings in the same
aspect, together with the empowering Deities.

DZA HUM BAM HO
They become non-dual.

Granting empowerment

The empowering Deities grant empowerment and his
crown is adorned by Akshobya.

Offering

OM VAJRADAKA SAPARIWARA AHRGHAM PARTITZA
    HUM SÖHA
OM VAJRADAKA SAPARIWARA PADÄM PARTITZA HUM
    SÖHA
OM VAJRADAKA SAPARIWARA PUPE PARTITZA HUM
    SÖHA

OM VAJRADAKA SAPARIWARA DHUPE PARTITZA HUM
    SÖHA

OM VAJRADAKA SAPARIWARA ALOKE PARTITZA HUM
    SÖHA

OM VAJRADAKA SAPARIWARA GÄNDHE PARTITZA HUM
    SÖHA

OM VAJRADAKA SAPARIWARA NEWIDE PARTITZA HUM
    SÖHA

OM VAJRADAKA SAPARIWARA SHAPTA PARTITZA HUM
    SÖHA

Prostration

O Vajra Akshobya, great exalted wisdom,
Great skilful one from the vajra sphere,
Supreme among the three vajras and three mandalas,
To you Vajradaka I prostrate.

Visualization for making the burning offering

I remain in my ordinary form. At my heart is a black
letter PAM, the seed of negativity. At my navel, from
RAM, comes a red fire mandala. On the soles of both my
feet, from YAM, comes a blue wind mandala.

Light rays radiate from the letter PAM and draw back all
the negativities and obstructions of my three doors in the
aspect of black rays of light. These dissolve into the PAM.

Below, the wind blows and enters through the soles
of my feet. The fire at my navel blazes and light rays
from the fire drive the PAM out through my nostrils.
My negativities take on the aspect of a scorpion, which

dissolves into the sesame seeds. I offer these to the mouth of Vajradaka.

OM VAJRA DAKA KHA KHA KHAHI KHAHI SARWA
PAPAM DAHANA BHAKMI KURU SÖHA

May all the negativities, obstructions, and degenerated commitments I have accumulated during beginningless lives in samsara [be purified] SHÄNTING KURUYE SÖHA

Offer the sesame seeds to Vajradaka while reciting the mantra and the brief request prayer. Continue in this way until all the sesame seeds have been offered.

Thanking offering

OM VAJRADAKA SAPARIWARA AHRGHAM , PADÄM,
PUPE, DHUPE, ALOKE, GÄNDHE, NEWIDE, SHAPTA
PARTITZA HUM SÖHA

Prostration

Merely by our remembering your dark-blue form of a
    wrathful cannibal,
Amidst a blazing mass of exalted wisdom fire,
You destroy all maras, negativities and obstructions;
To you Vajradaka I prostrate.

Requesting forbearance

Whatever mistakes I have made
Through not finding, not understanding,
Or not having the ability,
Please, O Protector, be patient with all of these.

Dissolution

The wisdom beings return to their natural abodes, and
the commitment being transforms into the aspect of a
blazing fire.

Dedication

By this virtue, throughout all my lives
May I never be parted from the Mahayana Guru who
    reveals the unmistaken path,
And by always remaining under his care
May I drink continuously from the nectar of his speech.

Due to this, may I and others complete the practices
Of renunciation, bodhichitta, correct view,
The six perfections, and the two stages,
And may we swiftly attain the state endowed with the
    ten powers.

Through the blessings of the non-deceptive Guru and
    Three Jewels,
And the power of the immutable nature of phenomena
    and non-deceptive dependent relationship,
May everything be auspicious for my excellent prayers
    to be accomplished
So that I may swiftly attain omniscient Buddhahood.

Colophon: This sadhana or ritual for spiritual attainments
was translated under the compassionate guidance of
Venerable Geshe Kelsang Gyatso Rinpoche.

Glossary

Akshobya The manifestation of the aggregate of consciousness of all Buddhas. He has a blue-coloured body.

Amitabha The manifestation of the aggregate of discrimination of all Buddhas. He has a red-coloured body.

Atisha (AD 982-1054) A famous Indian Buddhist scholar and meditation master. He was Abbot of the great Buddhist monastery of Vikramashila at a time when Mahayana Buddhism was flourishing in India. He was later invited to Tibet and his arrival there led to the re-establishment of Buddhism in Tibet. He is the author of the first text on the stages of the path, *Lamp for the Path to Enlightenment*. His tradition later became known as the 'Kadampa Tradition'. *See Joyful Path of Good Fortune.*

Attainment 'Siddhi' in Sanskrit. These are of two types: common attainments and supreme attainments. Common attainments are of four principal types: pacifying attainments (the ability to purify negativity, overcome obstacles and cure sickness), increasing attainments (the ability to increase Dharma realizations, merit, life span and wealth), controlling attainments (the ability to control one's own and others' minds and actions) and wrathful attainments (the ability to use wrathful actions where appropriate to benefit others). Supreme attainments are the special realizations of a Buddha. See *Tantric Grounds and Paths*.

Basis of imputation All phenomena are imputed upon their parts, therefore any of the individual parts, or the entire collection of the parts, of any phenomenon is its basis of imputation. A phenomenon is imputed by mind in dependence upon its basis of imputation appearing to that mind. See *The New Heart of Wisdom*.

Blessing   The transformation of our mind from a negative state to a positive state, from an unhappy state to a happy state, or from a state of weakness to a state of strength, through the inspiration of holy beings such as our Spiritual Guide, Buddhas and Bodhisattvas.

Bodhichitta   Sanskrit word for 'mind of enlightenment'. 'Bodhi' means 'enlightenment', and 'chitta' means 'mind'. There are two types of bodhichitta – conventional bodhichitta and ultimate bodhichitta. Generally speaking, the term 'bodhichitta' refers to conventional bodhichitta, which is a primary mind motivated by great compassion that spontaneously seeks enlightenment to benefit all living beings. There are two types of conventional bodhichitta – aspiring bodhichitta and engaging bodhichitta. Ultimate bodhichitta is a wisdom motivated by conventional bodhichitta that directly realizes emptiness, the ultimate nature of phenomena. See *Joyful Path of Good Fortune* and *Meaningful to Behold*.

Bodhisattva   A person who has generated spontaneous bodhichitta but who has not yet become a Buddha. See *Joyful Path of Good Fortune* and *Meaningful to Behold.*

Body mandala   The transformation into a Deity of any part of the body of a self-generated or in-front-generated Deity. See *The New Guide to Dakini Land, Great Treasury of Merit* and *Essence of Vajrayana.*

Brahma   A worldly god (Skt. deva). See *Ocean of Nectar.*

Buddha   A being who has completely abandoned all delusions and their imprints. See also *Buddha Shakyamuni*. See *Joyful Path of Good Fortune.*

Buddha family   There are five main Buddha families: the families of Vairochana, Ratnasambhava, Amitabha, Amoghasiddhi and Akshobya. They are the five purified aggregates – the aggregates of form, feeling, discrimination, compositional factors and consciousness, respectively; and the five exalted wisdoms – the exalted mirror-like wisdom, the exalted wisdom of equality, the exalted wisdom of individual realization, the exalted wisdom of accomplishing activities and the exalted wisdom of the Dharmadhatu, respectively. See *Great Treasury of Merit.*

Buddha Shakyamuni   The fourth of one thousand founding Buddhas who are to appear in this world during this Fortunate Aeon. The first three were Krakuchchanda, Kanakamuni and Kashyapa. The fifth Buddha will be Maitreya. See *Introduction to Buddhism*.

Central channel   The principal channel at the very centre of the body, along which the channel wheels are located. See *Clear Light of Bliss* and *Mahamudra Tantra*.

Channel wheel   'Chakra' in Sanskrit. A focal centre where secondary channels branch out from the central channel. Meditating on these points can cause the inner winds to enter the central channel. See *Clear Light of Bliss*.

Clear appearance   Generally, a clear perception of the object of meditation. More specifically, a Secret Mantra practice whereby the practitioner, having generated himself or herself as a Deity and the environment as the Deity's mandala, tries to attain clear appearance of the whole object to his or her concentration. It is the antidote to ordinary appearance. See *The New Guide to Dakini Land*.

Clear light   A manifest very subtle mind that perceives an appearance like clear, empty space. See *Clear Light of Bliss*.

Close retreat   A retreat during which we strive to draw close to a particular Deity. This can be understood in two ways: drawing close in the sense of developing a special relationship with a friend, and drawing close in the sense of becoming more and more like the Deity. An action close retreat is a close retreat in which we collect a certain number of mantras and conclude with a fire puja. See *The New Guide to Dakini Land*.

Collection of merit   A virtuous action motivated by bodhichitta that is a main cause of attaining the Form Body of a Buddha. Examples are: making offerings and prostrations to holy beings with bodhichitta motivation, and the practice of the perfections of giving, moral discipline, and patience.

Collection of wisdom   A virtuous mental action motivated by bodhichitta that is a main cause of attaining the Truth Body of a Buddha. Examples are: listening to, contemplating and meditating on emptiness with bodhichitta motivation.

Commitment being   A visualized Buddha or ourself visualized as a Buddha. A commitment being is so called because in general it is the commitment of all Buddhists to visualize or remember Buddha, and in particular it is a commitment of those who have received an empowerment into Highest Yoga Tantra to generate themselves as a Deity.

Compassion   A mind that cannot bear the suffering of others and wishes them to be free from it. See also *Great compassion*. See *Joyful Path of Good Fortune* and *Universal Compassion*.

Completion stage   Highest Yoga Tantra realizations developed in dependence upon the winds entering, abiding and dissolving within the central channel through the force of meditation. See *Tantric Grounds and Paths* and *Mahamudra Tantra*.

Contaminated aggregate   Any of the aggregates of form, feeling, discrimination, compositional factors, and consciousness of a samsaric being. See *The New Heart of Wisdom*.

Conventional truth   Any phenomenon other than emptiness. Conventional truths are true with respect to the minds of ordinary beings, but in reality they are false. See *The New Heart of Wisdom*.

Dakinis/Dakas   Dakinis are female Tantric Buddhas and those women who have attained the realization of meaning clear light. Dakas are the male equivalent. See *The New Guide to Dakini Land*.

Degenerate times   A period when spiritual activity degenerates.

Deity   'Yidam' in Tibetan. A Tantric enlightened being.

Demon   See *Mara/Demon*.

Desire realm   The environment of hell beings, hungry spirits, animals, human beings, demi-gods and the gods who enjoy the five objects of desire.

Dharmakaya   Sanskrit word for the Truth Body of a Buddha.

Dharmakirti   A great Indian Buddhist Yogi and scholar who composed *Commentary to Valid Cognition*, a commentary to *Compendium of Valid Cognition*, which was written by his Spiritual Guide, Dignaga. See *How to Understand the Mind*.

Divine pride A non-deluded pride that regards oneself as a Deity and one's environment and enjoyments as those of the Deity. It is the antidote to ordinary conceptions. See *The New Guide to Dakini Land* and *Mahamudra Tantra*.

Dualistic appearance The appearance to mind of an object together with the inherent existence of that object. See *The New Heart of Wisdom*.

Eight worldly concerns The objects of the eight worldly concerns are happiness and suffering, wealth and poverty, praise and criticism, and good reputation and bad reputation. These are called 'worldly concerns' because worldly people are constantly concerned with them, wanting some and trying to avoid others. See *Universal Compassion* and *Joyful Path of Good Fortune*.

Emanation Animate or inanimate form manifested by Buddhas or high Bodhisattvas to benefit others.

Emanation Body 'Nirmanakaya' in Sanskrit. A Buddha's Form Body that can be perceived by ordinary beings. See *Tantric Grounds and Paths*.

Empowerment A special potential power to attain any of the four Buddha bodies that is received by a Tantric practitioner from his or her Guru, or from other holy beings, by means of Tantric ritual. It is the gateway to the Vajrayana. See *Tantric Grounds and Paths*.

Emptiness Lack of inherent existence, the ultimate nature of phenomena. See *The New Heart of Wisdom* and *Transform Your Life*.

Enjoyment Body 'Sambhogakaya' in Sanskrit. A Buddha's subtle Form Body that can be perceived only by Mahayana Superiors. See *Tantric Grounds and Paths*.

Field for Accumulating Merit The Three Jewels. Just as external seeds grow in a field of soil, so the virtuous internal seeds produced by virtuous actions grow in dependence upon Buddha Jewel, Dharma Jewel, and Sangha Jewel. Also known as 'Field of Merit'.

Fortunate Aeon The name given to this world age. It is so called because one thousand founding Buddhas will appear during this aeon. Buddha Shakyamuni was the fourth and Buddha Maitreya will be the fifth. A 'Dark Aeon' is an aeon in which no Buddhas appear.

Four fearlessnesses Special qualities of a Buddha. A fearlessness is an utterly firm, ultimate realization that is entirely free from fear in expounding Dharma. See *Ocean of Nectar*.

Four maras See *Mara/Demon*.

Four noble truths True sufferings, true origins, true cessations and true paths. They are called 'noble' truths because they are supreme objects of meditation. Through meditation on these four objects, we can realize ultimate truth directly and thus become a noble, or Superior, being. Sometimes referred to as the 'four truths of Superiors'. See *Joyful Path of Good Fortune* and *How to Solve Our Human Problems*.

Generation stage A realization of a creative yoga prior to attaining the actual completion stage, which is attained through the practice of bringing the three bodies into the path, in which one mentally generates oneself as a Tantric Deity and one's surroundings as the Deity's mandala. Meditation on generation stage is called a 'creative yoga' because its object is created, or generated, by correct imagination. See *Tantric Grounds and Paths* and *Mahamudra Tantra*.

Generic image The appearing object of a conceptual mind. The conceptual mind mistakes the generic image, or mental image, for the object itself. For example, if we think about our mother, an image of our mother appears to our conceptual mind, and it seems to that mind as if our mother herself is appearing. However, the object that principally appears to that mind is the generic image of our mother. This generic image appears to our mind through the mental exclusion of all objects that are not our mother. It is therefore the appearance of a non-non-mother. See *How to Understand the Mind*.

Great compassion A mind wishing to protect all sentient beings from suffering. See *Universal Compassion* and *Transform Your Life*.

Great fault, the The fault of rejecting Dharma as a result of wrongly discriminating between Buddha's scriptures. See *Joyful Path of Good Fortune*.

Guru See *Root Guru* and *Spiritual Guide*.

Heruka A principal Deity of Mother Tantra, who is the embodiment of indivisible bliss and emptiness. He has a blue-coloured body, four faces and twelve arms, and embraces his consort Vajravarahi. See *Essence of Vajrayana* and *Modern Buddhism*.

Highest Yoga Tantra   A Tantric instruction that includes the method for transforming sexual bliss into the spiritual path. See *Tantric Grounds and Paths* and *Mahamudra Tantra*.

Hinayana   Sanskrit word for 'Lesser Vehicle'. The Hinayana goal is to attain merely one's own liberation from suffering by completely abandoning delusions. See *Joyful Path of Good Fortune*.

Ignorance   A mental factor that is confused about the ultimate nature of phenomena. See *How to Understand the Mind*.

Illusory body   The subtle divine body that is principally developed from the indestructible wind. When a practitioner of Highest Yoga Tantra rises from the meditation of the isolated mind of ultimate example clear light, he or she attains a body that is not the same as his or her ordinary physical body. This new body is the illusory body. It has the same appearance as the body of the personal Deity of generation stage except that it is white in colour, and it can be perceived only by those who have already attained an illusory body. See *Clear Light of Bliss* and *Tantric Grounds and Paths*.

Indra   A worldly god (Skt. deva). See *The New Heart of Wisdom.*

Inherent existence   An imagined mode of existence whereby phenomena are held to exist from their own side, independent of other phenomena. In reality, all phenomena are empty of inherent existence because they depend upon their parts. See *The New Heart of Wisdom*.

Kadampa   A Tibetan word in which 'Ka' means 'word' and refers to all Buddha's teachings, 'dam' refers to Atisha's special Lamrim instructions known as the 'stages of the path to enlightenment', and 'pa' refers to a follower of Kadampa Buddhism who integrates all the teachings of Buddha that they know into their Lamrim practice. See also *Kadampa Buddhism* and *Kadampa Tradition*.

Kadampa Buddhism   A Mahayana Buddhist school founded by the great Indian Buddhist Master Atisha (AD 982-1054). See also *Kadampa* and *Kadampa Tradition*.

Kadampa Tradition   The pure tradition of Buddhism established by Atisha. Followers of this tradition up to the time of Je Tsongkhapa are known as 'Old Kadampas', and those after the time of Je Tsongkhapa are known as 'New Kadampas'. See also *Kadampa* and *Kadampa Buddhism*.

Kalarupa   A Dharma Protector who is an emanation of Manjushri.

Kangyur   The collection of all the Sutras and Tantras that have been translated from Sanskrit into Tibetan. See also *Tengyur*.

Lamrim   A Tibetan term, literally meaning 'stages of the path'. A special arrangement of all Buddha's teachings that is easy to understand and put into practice. It reveals all the stages of the path to enlightenment. For a full commentary, see *Joyful Path of Good Fortune.*

Liberation   'Nirvana' in Sanskrit. Complete freedom from samsara and its cause, the delusions. See *Joyful Path of Good Fortune*.

Lineage   A line of instruction that has been passed down from Spiritual Guide to disciple, with each Spiritual Guide in the line having gained personal experience of the instruction before passing it on to others.

Lojong   A Tibetan term, literally meaning 'training the mind'. A special lineage of instructions that came from Buddha Shakyamuni through Manjushri and Shantideva to Atisha and the Kadampa Geshes, which emphasizes the generation of bodhichitta through the practices of equalizing and exchanging self with others combined with taking and giving. See *Universal Compassion* and *Eight Steps to Happiness.*

Losang Dragpa   'Sumati Kirti' in Sanskrit. The ordained name of Je Tsongkhapa. See *Great Treasury of Merit*.

Madhyamika   A Sanskrit word, literally meaning 'Middle Way'. The higher of the two schools of Mahayana tenets. The Madhyamika view was taught by Buddha in the *Perfection of Wisdom Sutras* during the second turning of the Wheel of Dharma and was subsequently elucidated by Nagarjuna and his followers. There are two divisions of this school, Madhyamika-Svatantrika and Madhyamika-Prasangika, of which the latter is Buddha's final view. See *Meaningful to Behold* and *Ocean of Nectar*.

Mahakala   A Dharma Protector who appears in many different aspects – four-armed, six-armed, four-faced and so forth.

Mahamudra   A Sanskrit word, literally meaning 'great seal'. According to Sutra, this refers to the profound view of emptiness. Since emptiness is the nature of all phenomena, it is called a 'seal', and since a direct realization of emptiness enables us to accomplish the great purpose – complete liberation from the sufferings of samsara

– it is also called 'great'. According to Secret Mantra, great seal is the union of spontaneous great bliss and emptiness. See *Mahamudra Tantra*, *The Oral Instructions of Mahamudra* and *Clear Light of Bliss*.

Mahasiddha   Sanskrit word for 'greatly accomplished one', which is used to refer to Yogis or Yoginis with high attainments.

Mahayana   Sanskrit word for 'Great Vehicle', the spiritual path to great enlightenment. The Mahayana goal is to attain Buddhahood for the benefit of all living beings by completely abandoning delusions and their imprints. See *Joyful Path of Good Fortune*.

Maitreya   The embodiment of the loving kindness of all the Buddhas. At the time of Buddha Shakyamuni, he manifested as a Bodhisattva disciple. In the future, he will manifest as the fifth founding Buddha.

Mandala offering   An offering of the entire universe visualized as a Pure Land, with all its inhabitants as pure beings. See *The New Guide to Dakini Land*.

Mantra   A Sanskrit word, literally meaning 'mind protection'. Mantra protects the mind from ordinary appearances and conceptions. There are four types of mantra: mantras that are mind, mantras that are inner wind, mantras that are sound, and mantras that are form. In general, there are three types of mantra recitation: verbal recitation, mental recitation, and vajra recitation. See *Tantric Grounds and Paths*.

Mara/Demon   'Mara' is Sanskrit for 'demon', and refers to anything that obstructs the attainment of liberation or enlightenment. There are four principal types of mara: the mara of the delusions, the mara of contaminated aggregates, the mara of uncontrolled death and the Devaputra maras. Of these, only the last are actual living beings. The principal Devaputra mara is wrathful Ishvara, the highest of the desire realm gods, who inhabits Land of Controlling Emanations. Buddha is called a 'Conqueror' because he or she has conquered all four types of mara. See *The New Heart of Wisdom*.

Meditative equipoise   Single-pointed concentration on a virtuous object such as emptiness. See *Mahamudra Tantra* and *Meaningful to Behold*.

Merit   The good fortune created by virtuous actions. It is the potential power to increase our good qualities and produce happiness.

Moral discipline   A virtuous mental determination to abandon any fault, or a bodily or verbal action motivated by such a determination. See *Joyful Path of Good Fortune*.

Mount Meru   According to Buddhist cosmology, a divine mountain that stands at the centre of the universe.

Nalanda Monastery   A great seat of Buddhist learning and practice in ancient India.

Nirvana   See *Liberation*.

Non-virtuous actions   Non-virtuous actions are countless, but most of them are included within ten: killing, stealing, sexual misconduct, lying, divisive speech, hurtful speech, idle gossip, covetousness, malice and holding wrong views. See *Joyful Path of Good Fortune*.

Obstructions to liberation   Obstructions that prevent the attainment of liberation. All delusions, such as ignorance, attachment and anger, together with their seeds, are obstructions to liberation. Also called 'delusion-obstructions'.

Obstructions to omniscience   The imprints of delusions that prevent simultaneous and direct realization of all phenomena. Only Buddhas have overcome these obstructions.

Offering to the Spiritual Guide   *Lama Chopa* in Tibetan. A special Guru yoga of Je Tsongkhapa, in which our Spiritual Guide is visualized in the aspect of Lama Losang Tubwang Dorjechang. The instruction for this practice was revealed by Buddha Manjushri in the *Kadam Emanation Scripture* and written down by the first Panchen Lama. It is an essential preliminary practice for Vajrayana Mahamudra. For a full commentary, see *Great Treasury of Merit*.

Ordinary appearance and conception   Ordinary appearance is any appearance that is due to an impure mind, and ordinary conception is any mind that conceives things as ordinary. According to Tantra, ordinary appearances are obstructions to omniscience and ordinary conceptions are obstructions to liberation. See *Mahamudra Tantra* and *Tantric Grounds and Paths*.

Perfection of Wisdom Sutras   Sutras of the second turning of the Wheel of Dharma, in which Buddha revealed his final view of the ultimate nature of all phenomena – emptiness of inherent existence. See *The New Heart of Wisdom* and *Ocean of Nectar*.

Pratimoksha   Sanskrit word for 'individual liberation'. See *The Bodhisattva Vow*.

Profound path   The profound path includes all the wisdom practices that lead to a direct realization of emptiness and ultimately to the Truth Body of a Buddha. See *Joyful Path of Good Fortune* and *Ocean of Nectar*.

Puja   A ceremony in which offerings and other acts of devotion are performed in front of holy beings.

Pure Land   A pure environment in which there are no true sufferings. There are many Pure Lands. For example, Tushita is the Pure Land of Buddha Maitreya, Sukhavati is the Pure Land of Buddha Amitabha, and Dakini Land, or Keajra, is the Pure Land of Buddha Vajrayogini and Buddha Heruka. See *Living Meaningfully, Dying Joyfully*.

Renunciation   The wish to be released from samsara. See *Joyful Path of Good Fortune*.

Root Guru   The principal Spiritual Guide from whom we have received the empowerments, instructions and oral transmissions of our main practice. See *Great Treasury of Merit* and *Joyful Path of Good Fortune*.

Sadhana   A ritual that is a method for attaining spiritual realizations. It can be associated with Sutra or Tantra.

Samsara   This can be understood in two ways – as uninterrupted rebirth without freedom or control, or as the aggregates of a being who has taken such a rebirth. Samsara is characterized by suffering and dissatisfaction. There are six realms of samsara. Listed in ascending order according to the type of karma that causes rebirth in them, they are the realms of the hell beings, hungry spirits, animals, humans beings, demi-gods and gods. The first three are lower realms or unhappy migrations, and the second three are higher realms or happy migrations. Although from the point of view of the karma that causes rebirth there, the god realm is the highest realm in samsara, the human realm is said to be the most fortunate realm because it provides the best conditions for attaining liberation and enlightenment. See *Joyful Path of Good Fortune*.

Sangha   According to the Vinaya tradition, any community of four or more fully ordained monks or nuns. In general, ordained or lay people who take Bodhisattva vows or Tantric vows can also be said to be Sangha.

Secret Mantra   Synonymous with Tantra. Secret Mantra teachings are distinguished from Sutra teachings in that they reveal methods for training the mind by bringing the future result, or Buddhahood, into the present path. Secret Mantra is the supreme path to full enlightenment. See *Tantric Grounds and Paths*.

Seed-letter   The sacred letter from which a Deity is generated. Each Deity has a particular seed-letter.

Self-cherishing   A mental attitude that considers oneself to be supremely important and precious. It is regarded as a principal object to be abandoned by Bodhisattvas. See *Eight Steps to Happiness* and *Meaningful to Behold*.

Self-grasping   A conceptual mind that holds any phenomenon to be inherently existent. The mind of self-grasping gives rise to all other delusions, such as anger and attachment. It is the root cause of all suffering and dissatisfaction. See *The New Heart of Wisdom* and *Ocean of Nectar*.

Signs and indications   Special characteristics of a Buddha's form. Examples of the thirty-two major signs, or 'major marks', are the sign of the wheel on the palms of the hands and the soles of the feet. The eighty indications, sometimes called the 'minor marks', include signs such as copper-coloured nails.

Six perfections   The perfections of giving, moral discipline, patience, effort, mental stabilization and wisdom. They are called 'perfections' because they are motivated by bodhichitta. See *Joyful Path of Good Fortune* and *Meaningful to Behold*.

Six realms   See *Samsara*.

Spiritual Guide   'Guru' in Sanskrit, 'Lama' in Tibetan. A Teacher who guides us along the spiritual path. See *Joyful Path of Good Fortune* and *Great Treasury of Merit*.

Stages of the path   See *Lamrim*.

Superior being   'Arya' in Sanskrit. A being who has a direct realization of emptiness. There are Hinayana Superiors and Mahayana Superiors.

Superior seeing   A special wisdom that sees its object clearly, and that is maintained by tranquil abiding and the special suppleness that is induced by investigation. See *Joyful Path of Good Fortune*.

Supreme Emanation Body   A special Emanation Body displaying the thirty-two major signs and eighty minor indications that can be seen by ordinary beings only if they have very pure karma. See also *Emanation Body*.

Sutra   The teachings of Buddha that are open to everyone to practise without the need for empowerment. These include Buddha's teachings of the three turnings of the Wheel of Dharma.

Tengyur   The collection of commentaries to Buddha's teachings that have been translated from Sanskrit into Tibetan. See also *Kangyur*.

Ten directions   The four cardinal directions, the four intermediate directions, and the directions above and below.

Three Jewels   The three objects of refuge: Buddha Jewel, Dharma Jewel, and Sangha Jewel. They are called 'Jewels' because they are both rare and precious. See *Joyful Path of Good Fortune*.

Three realms   The three levels within samsara: the desire realm, the form realm and the formless realm.

Torma offering   A special food offering made according to either Sutric or Tantric rituals. See *Essence of Vajrayana*.

Training the mind   See *Lojong*.

Tranquil abiding   A concentration that possesses the special bliss of physical and mental suppleness that is attained in dependence upon completing the nine mental abidings. See *Joyful Path of Good Fortune* and *Meaningful to Behold*.

Transference of consciousness   'Powa' in Tibetan. A practice for transferring the consciousness to a Pure Land at the time of death. See *Living Meaningfully, Dying Joyfully*.

True cessation   The ultimate nature of a mind freed from any obstruction by means of a true path. See *Joyful Path of Good Fortune*.

True origin   An action or a delusion that is the main cause of a true suffering. See *Joyful Path of Good Fortune*.

True path   A spiritual path held by a wisdom directly realizing emptiness. See *Joyful Path of Good Fortune*.

True suffering A contaminated object produced by delusions and karma. See *Joyful Path of Good Fortune*.

Tsog offering An offering made by an assembly of Heroes and Heroines. See *The New Guide to Dakini Land*.

Two collections The collections of merit and wisdom. See *Collection of merit* and *Collection of wisdom*.

Ultimate truth The ultimate nature of all phenomena, emptiness. See *The New Heart of Wisdom* and *Transform Your Life*.

Uncontaminated bliss A realization of bliss conjoined with a wisdom directly realizing emptiness. See *The New Guide to Dakini Land* and *Tantric Grounds and Paths*.

Union of No More Learning A union of the pure illusory body and meaning clear light that has abandoned the obstructions to omniscience. Synonymous with Buddhahood. See *Clear Light of Bliss* and *Tantric Grounds and Paths*.

Union that needs learning A union of the pure illusory body and meaning clear light that has not yet abandoned the obstructions to omniscience. See *Clear Light of Bliss* and *Tantric Grounds and Paths*.

Unobservable compassion Compassion induced and accompanied by a realization that all living beings lack inherent existence. See *Ocean of Nectar*.

Vajra body Generally, the channels, drops and inner winds. More specifically, the pure illusory body. The body of a Buddha is known as the 'resultant vajra body'. See *Clear Light of Bliss*.

Vajradaka Burning Offering A special purification practice in which our negativities and downfalls are transformed into black sesame seeds, which are offered to Vajradaka who appears from a blazing fire to consume them.

Vajradhara The founder of Vajrayana. He is the same mental continuum as Buddha Shakyamuni but displays a different aspect. Buddha Shakyamuni appears in the aspect of an Emanation Body, and Conqueror Vajradhara appears in the aspect of an Enjoyment Body. See *Great Treasury of Merit*.

Vajrapani The embodiment of the power of all the Buddhas. He appears in a wrathful aspect, displaying his power to overcome outer, inner and secret obstacles.

Vajra posture   The perfect cross-legged posture. See *Joyful Path of Good Fortune.*

Vajrayana   The Secret Mantra vehicle. See *Tantric Grounds and Paths.*

Vajrayogini   A female Highest Yoga Tantra Deity who is the embodiment of indivisible bliss and emptiness. She is the same nature as Heruka. See *The New Guide to Dakini Land.*

Vast path   The vast path includes all the method practices from the initial cultivation of compassion through to the final attainment of the Form Body of a Buddha. See *Joyful Path of Good Fortune* and *Ocean of Nectar.*

Vinaya Sutras   Sutras in which Buddha principally explains the practice of moral discipline, and in particular the Pratimoksha moral discipline.

Vows   Promises to refrain from certain actions. The three sets of vows are the Pratimoksha vows of individual liberation, the Bodhisattva vows, and the Secret Mantra vows. See *The Bodhisattva Vow* and *Tantric Grounds and Paths.*

Wheel of Dharma   Buddha gave his teachings in three main phases, which are known as 'the three turnings of the Wheel of Dharma'. During the first Wheel he taught the four noble truths, during the second he taught the *Perfection of Wisdom Sutras* and revealed the Madhyamika-Prasangika view, and during the third he taught the Chittamatra view. See *Introduction to Buddhism.*

Wisdom   A virtuous, intelligent mind that makes its primary mind realize its object thoroughly. A wisdom is a spiritual path that functions to release our mind from delusions or their imprints. An example of wisdom is the correct view of emptiness. See *The New Heart of Wisdom* and *How to Understand the Mind.*

Wisdom being   An actual Buddha, especially one who is invited to unite with a visualized commitment being.

Yamantaka   A Highest Yoga Tantra Deity who is a wrathful manifestation of Manjushri.

Yidam   See *Deity.*

Bibliography

Venerable Geshe Kelsang Gyatso Rinpoche is a highly respected meditation master and scholar of the Mahayana Buddhist tradition founded by Je Tsongkhapa. Since arriving in the West in 1977, Venerable Geshe Kelsang has worked tirelessly to establish pure Buddhadharma throughout the world. Over this period he has given extensive teachings on the major scriptures of the Mahayana. These teachings provide a comprehensive presentation of the essential Sutra and Tantra practices of Mahayana Buddhism.

Books

The following books by Venerable Geshe Kelsang Gyatso Rinpoche are all published by Tharpa Publications.

The Bodhisattva Vow A practical guide to helping others.
(2nd. edn., 1995)

Clear Light of Bliss A Tantric meditation manual. (3rd. edn., 2014)

Eight Steps to Happiness The Buddhist way of loving kindness. (2nd. edn., 2012)

Essence of Vajrayana The Highest Yoga Tantra practice of Heruka body mandala. (1997)

Great Treasury of Merit How to rely upon a Spiritual Guide. (2nd. edn., 2015)

Guide to the Bodhisattva's Way of Life How to enjoy a life of great meaning and altruism. (A translation of Shantideva's famous verse masterpiece.) (2002)

Heart Jewel The essential practices of Kadampa Buddhism. (2nd. edn., 1997)

How to Solve Our Human Problems The four noble truths. (2005)

How to Understand the Mind The nature and power of the mind. (4th. edn., 2014)

Introduction to Buddhism An explanation of the Buddhist way of life. (2nd. edn., 2001)

Joyful Path of Good Fortune The complete Buddhist path to enlightenment. (2nd. edn., 1995)

Living Meaningfully, Dying Joyfully The profound practice of transference of consciousness. (1999)

Mahamudra Tantra The supreme Heart Jewel nectar. (2005)

Meaningful to Behold Becoming a friend of the world. (5th. edn., 2007)

Modern Buddhism The path of compassion and wisdom. (2nd. edn., 2013)

The New Guide to Dakini Land The Highest Yoga Tantra practice of Buddha Vajrayogini. (3rd. edn., 2012)

The New Heart of Wisdom Profound teachings from Buddha's heart (An explanation of the *Heart Sutra*). (5th. edn., 2012)

The New Meditation Handbook Meditations to make our life happy and meaningful. (5th. edn., 2013)

Ocean of Nectar The true nature of all things. (1995)

The Oral Instruction of Mahamudra The very essence of Buddha's teachings of Sutra and Tantra. (2nd. edn., 2016)

Tantric Grounds and Paths How to enter, progress on, and complete the Vajrayana path. (1994)

Transform Your Life A blissful journey. (2nd. edn., 2014)

Universal Compassion Inspiring solutions for difficult times. (4th. edn., 2002)

Sadhanas and Other Booklets

Venerable Geshe Kelsang Gyatso Rinpoche has also supervised the translation of a collection of essential sadhanas, or ritual prayers for spiritual attainments, available in booklet or audio formats.

Avalokiteshvara Sadhana Prayers and requests to the Buddha of Compassion.

The Blissful Path The condensed self-generation sadhana of Vajrayogini.

The Bodhisattva's Confession of Moral Downfalls The purification practice of the *Mahayana Sutra of the Three Superior Heaps*.

Condensed Essence of Vajrayana Condensed Heruka body mandala self-generation sadhana.

Condensed Long Life Practice of Buddha Amitayus

Dakini Yoga The middling self-generation sadhana of Vajrayogini.

Drop of Essential Nectar A special fasting and purification practice in conjunction with Eleven-faced Avalokiteshvara.

Essence of Good Fortune Prayers for the six preparatory practices for meditation on the stages of the path to enlightenment.

Essence of Vajrayana Heruka body mandala self-generation sadhana according to the system of Mahasiddha Ghantapa.

Feast of Great Bliss Vajrayogini self-initiation sadhana.

Great Liberation of the Father Preliminary prayers for Mahamudra meditation in conjunction with Heruka practice.

Great Liberation of the Mother Preliminary prayers for Mahamudra meditation in conjunction with Vajrayogini practice.

The Great Mother A method to overcome hindrances and obstacles by reciting the *Essence of Wisdom Sutra* (the *Heart Sutra*)

A Handbook for the Daily Practice of Bodhisattva and Tantric Vows.

Heartfelt Prayers Funeral service for cremations and burials.

Heart Jewel The Guru yoga of Je Tsongkhapa combined with the condensed sadhana of his Dharma Protector.

The Kadampa Way of Life The essential practice of Kadam Lamrim.

Keajra Heaven The essential commentary to the practice of *The Uncommon Yoga of Inconceivability*.

Lay Pratimoksha Vow Ceremony

Liberating Prayer Praise to Buddha Shakyamuni

Liberation from Sorrow Praises and requests to the Twenty-one Taras.

Mahayana Refuge Ceremony and Bodhisattva Vow Ceremony.

Medicine Buddha Prayer A method for benefiting others.

Medicine Buddha Sadhana A method for accomplishing the attainments of Medicine Buddha.

Meditation and Recitation of Solitary Vajrasattva.

Melodious Drum Victorious in all Directions The extensive fulfilling and restoring ritual of the Dharma Protector, the great king Dorje Shugden, in conjunction with Mahakala, Kalarupa, Kalindewi and other Dharma Protectors.

Offering to the Spiritual Guide (*Lama Chopa*) A special way of relying upon a Spiritual Guide.

Path of Compassion for the Deceased Powa sadhana for the benefit of the deceased.

Pathway to the Pure Land Training in powa – the transference of consciousness.

Powa Ceremony Transference of consciousness for the deceased.

Prayers for Meditation Brief preparatory prayers for meditation.

Prayers for World Peace.

A Pure Life The practice of taking and keeping the eight Mahayana precepts.

Quick Path to Great Bliss The extensive self-generation sadhana of Vajrayogini.

The Root Tantra of Heruka and Vajrayogini Chapters One & Fifty-one of the *Condensed Heruka Root Tantra*.

The Root Text: Eight Verses of Training the Mind.

Treasury of Wisdom The sadhana of Venerable Manjushri.

215

The Uncommon Yoga of Inconceivability The special instruction of how to reach the Pure Land of Keajra with this human body

Union of No More Learning Heruka body mandala self-initiation sadhana.

The Vows and Commitments of Kadampa Buddhism.

Wishfulfilling Jewel The Guru yoga of Je Tsongkhapa combined with the sadhana of his Dharma Protector.

The Yoga of Buddha Amitayus A special method for increasing lifespan, wisdom and merit.

The Yoga of Buddha Heruka The essential self-generation sadhana of Heruka body mandala & Condensed six-session yoga.

The Yoga of Buddha Maitreya Self-generation sadhana.

The Yoga of Buddha Vajrapani Self-generation sadhana.

The Yoga of Enlightened Mother Arya Tara Self-generation sadhana.

The Yoga of Great Mother Prajnaparamita Self-generation sadhana.

The Yoga of Thousand-armed Avalokiteshvara Self-generation sadhana.

The Yoga of White Tara, Buddha of Long Life.

To order any of our publications, or to request a catalogue, please visit www.tharpa.com or contact your nearest Tharpa office listed on pages 222–223.

NKT-IKBU

Study Programmes of
Kadampa Buddhism

Kadampa Buddhism is a Mahayana Buddhist school founded by the great Indian Buddhist Master Atisha (AD 982-1054). His followers are known as 'Kadampas'. 'Ka' means 'word' and refers to Buddha's teachings, and 'dam' refers to Atisha's special Lamrim instructions known as 'the stages of the path to enlightenment'. By integrating their knowledge of all Buddha's teachings into their practice of Lamrim, and by integrating this into their everyday lives, Kadampa Buddhists are encouraged to use Buddha's teachings as practical methods for transforming daily activities into the path to enlightenment. The great Kadampa Teachers are famous not only for being great scholars but also for being spiritual practitioners of immense purity and sincerity.

The lineage of these teachings, both their oral transmission and blessings, was then passed from Teacher to disciple, spreading throughout much of Asia, and now to many countries throughout the Western world. Buddha's teachings, which are known as 'Dharma', are likened to a wheel that moves from country to country in accordance with changing conditions and people's karmic inclinations. The external forms of presenting Buddhism may change as it meets with different cultures and societies, but its essential authenticity is ensured through the continuation of an unbroken lineage of realized practitioners.

Kadampa Buddhism was first introduced into the West in 1977 by the renowned Buddhist Master, Venerable Geshe Kelsang Gyatso Rinpoche. Since that time, he has worked tirelessly to spread Kadampa Buddhism throughout the world by giving extensive teachings, writing many profound texts on Kadampa Buddhism, and founding the New Kadampa Tradition – International Kadampa Buddhist Union (NKT-IKBU), which now has over a thousand Kadampa Buddhist Centres worldwide. Each Centre offers study programmes on Buddhist psychology, philosophy and meditation instruction, as well as retreats for all levels of practitioner. The emphasis is on integrating Buddha's teachings into daily life to solve our human problems and to spread lasting peace and happiness throughout the world.

The Kadampa Buddhism of the NKT-IKBU is an entirely independent Buddhist tradition and has no political affiliations. It is an association of Buddhist Centres and practitioners that derive their inspiration and guidance from the example of the ancient Kadampa Buddhist Masters and their teachings, as presented by Venerable Geshe Kelsang.

There are three reasons why we need to study and practise the teachings of Buddha: to develop our wisdom, to cultivate a good heart, and to maintain a peaceful state of mind. If we do not strive to develop our wisdom, we will always remain ignorant of ultimate truth – the true nature of reality. Although we wish for happiness, our ignorance leads us to engage in non-virtuous actions, which are the main cause of all our suffering. If we do not cultivate a good heart, our selfish motivation destroys harmony and good relationships with others. We have no peace, and no chance to gain pure happiness. Without inner peace, outer peace is impossible. If we do not maintain a peaceful state of mind, we are not happy even if we have ideal conditions. On the other hand, when our mind is peaceful, we are happy, even if our external conditions are unpleasant. Therefore, the development of these qualities is of utmost importance for our daily happiness.

Venerable Geshe Kelsang, or 'Geshe-la' as he is affectionately called by his students, has designed three special spiritual programmes for the systematic study and practice of Kadampa Buddhism that are especially suited to the modern world – the General Programme (GP), the Foundation Programme (FP), and the Teacher Training Programme (TTP).

GENERAL PROGRAMME

The General Programme provides a basic introduction to Buddhist view, meditation and practice that is suitable for beginners. It also includes advanced teachings and practice from both Sutra and Tantra.

FOUNDATION PROGRAMME

The Foundation Programme provides an opportunity to deepen our understanding and experience of Buddhism through a systematic study of six texts:

1 *Joyful Path of Good Fortune* – a commentary to Atisha's Lamrim instructions, the stages of the path to enlightenment.
2 *Universal Compassion* – a commentary to Bodhisattva Chekhawa's *Training the Mind in Seven Points*.
3 *Eight Steps to Happiness* – a commentary to Bodhisattva Langri Tangpa's *Eight Verses of Training the Mind*.
4 *The New Heart of Wisdom* – a commentary to the *Heart Sutra*.
5 *Meaningful to Behold* – a commentary to Bodhisattva Shantideva's *Guide to the Bodhisattva's Way of Life*.
6 *How to Understand the Mind* – a detailed explanation of the mind, based on the works of the Buddhist scholars Dharmakirti and Dignaga.

The benefits of studying and practising these texts are as follows:

219

(1) *Joyful Path of Good Fortune* – we gain the ability to put all Buddha's teachings of both Sutra and Tantra into practice. We can easily make progress on, and complete, the stages of the path to the supreme happiness of enlightenment. From a practical point of view, Lamrim is the main body of Buddha's teachings, and the other teachings are like its limbs.

(2) and (3) *Universal Compassion* and *Eight Steps to Happiness* – we gain the ability to integrate Buddha's teachings into our daily life and solve all our human problems.

(4) *The New Heart of Wisdom* – we gain a realization of the ultimate nature of reality. By gaining this realization, we can eliminate the ignorance of self-grasping, which is the root of all our suffering.

(5) *Meaningful to Behold* – we transform our daily activities into the Bodhisattva's way of life, thereby making every moment of our human life meaningful.

(6) *How to Understand the Mind* – we understand the relationship between our mind and its external objects. If we understand that objects depend upon the subjective mind, we can change the way objects appear to us by changing our own mind. Gradually, we will gain the ability to control our mind and in this way solve all our problems.

TEACHER TRAINING PROGRAMME

The Teacher Training Programme is designed for people who wish to train as authentic Dharma Teachers. In addition to completing the study of fourteen texts of Sutra and Tantra, which include the six texts mentioned above, the student is required to observe certain commitments with regard to behaviour and way of life, and to complete a number of meditation retreats.

A Special Teacher Training Programme is also held at KMC London, and can be studied at the centre or by correspondence.

This special meditation and study programme consists of six courses spread over three years based on the books of Venerable Geshe Kelsang: *How to Understand the Mind*; *Modern Buddhism*; *The New Heart of Wisdom*; *Tantric Grounds and Paths*; Shantideva's *Guide to the Bodhisattva's Way of Life* and its commentary, *Meaningful to Behold*; and *Ocean of Nectar*.

All Kadampa Buddhist Centres are open to the public. Every year we celebrate Festivals in many countries throughout the world, including two in England, where people gather from around the world to receive special teachings and empowerments and to enjoy a spiritual holiday. Please feel free to visit us at any time!

For further information about NKT-IKBU study programmes or to find your nearest centre visit www.kadampa.org, or please contact:

NKT-IKBU Central Office
Conishead Priory
Ulverston, Cumbria,
LA12 9QQ, UK
Tel: +44 (0) 01229-588533
Email: info@kadampa.org
Website: www.kadampa.org

or

US NKT-IKBU Office
KMC New York
47 Sweeney Road
Glen Spey, NY 12737, USA
Tel: +1 845-856-9000

or

877-523-2672 (toll-free)
Fax: +1 845-856-2110
Email: info@kadampanewyork.org
Website: www.kadampanewyork.org

Tharpa Offices Worldwide

Tharpa books are currently published in English (UK and US), Chinese, French, German, Italian, Japanese, Portuguese and Spanish. Most languages are available from any Tharpa office listed

UK Office
Tharpa Publications UK
Conishead Priory
ULVERSTON
Cumbria, LA12 9QQ, UK
Tel: +44 (0)1229-588599
Web: tharpa.com/uk
E-mail: info.uk@tharpa.com

US Office
Tharpa Publications US
47 Sweeney Road
GLEN SPEY, NY 12737, USA
Tel: +1 845-856-5102
Toll-free: +1 888-741-3475
Fax: +1 845-856-2110
Web: tharpa.com/us
E-mail: info.us@tharpa.com

Asia Office
Tharpa Asia
1st Floor Causeway Tower,
16-22 Causeway Road,
Causeway Bay,
HONG KONG
Tel: +(852) 2507 2237
Web: tharpa.com/hk-en
E-mail: info.asia@tharpa.com

Australian Office
Tharpa Publications Australia
25 McCarthy Road,
MONBULK VIC 3793
AUSTRALIA
Tel: +61 (0)3 9756 7203
Web: tharpa.com/au
E-mail: info.au@tharpa.com

Brazilian Office
Editora Tharpa Brasil
Rua Artur de Azevedo 1360
Pinheiros, 05404-003
SÃO PAULO, SP, BRASIL
Tel: +55 (11) 3476-2330
Web: tharpa.com.br
E-mail: contato.br@tharpa.com

Canadian Office
Tharpa Publications Canada
631 Crawford St.,
TORONTO, ON M6G 3K1
CANADA
Tel: (+1) 416-762-8710
Toll-free: (+1) 866-523-2672
Fax: (+1) 416-762-2267
Web (Eng): tharpa.com/ca
Web (Fr): tharpa.com/ca-fr
E-mail: info.ca@tharpa.com

French Office
Editions Tharpa
Château de Segrais
72220 SAINT-MARS-
 D'OUTILLÉ, FRANCE
Tél/Fax : +33 (0)2 43 87 71 02
Web: tharpa.com/fr
E-mail: info.fr@tharpa.com

German Office
Tharpa-Verlag Deutschland
Mehringdamm 33, Aufgang 2,
10961 BERLIN, GERMANY
Tel: +49 (030) 430 55 666
Web: tharpa.com/de
E-mail: info.de@tharpa.com

Japanese Office
Tharpa Japan
KMC Tokyo
Web: kadampa.jp
E-mail: info@kadampa.jp

Mexican Office
Tharpa México
Enrique Rébsamen Nº 406,
Col. Narvate, entre Xola y
 Diagonal de San Antonio
MÉXICO D.F., C.P. 03020,
MÉXICO
Tel: +01 (55) 56 39 61 86
Tel: +01 (55) 56 39 61 80
Web: tharpa.com/mx
E-mail: tharpa@kadampa.org.mx

Portuguese Office
Publicações Tharpa Portugal
Rua Moinho do Gato, 5
Várzea de Sintra
2710-661 SINTRA
PORTUGAL
Tel: +351 219231064
Web: tharpa.pt
E-mail: info.pt@tharpa.com

South African Office
26 Menston Rd., Dawncliffe,
Westville, 3629, KZN,
REP. OF SOUTH AFRICA
Tel: +27 (0)72 551 3429
Fax: +27 (0)86 513 3476
Web: tharpa.com/za
E-mail: info.za@tharpa.com

Spanish Office
Editorial Tharpa España
Calle Manuela Malasaña 26
local dcha, 28004 MADRID,
SPAIN
Tel: +34 917 55 75 35
Web: tharpa.com/es
E-mail: info.es@tharpa.com

Swiss Office
Tharpa Verlag Schweiz
Mirabellenstrasse 1
CH-8048 ZÜRICH
SWITZERLAND
Tel: +41 44 401 02 20
Fax: +41 44 461 36 88
Web: tharpa.com/ch
E-mail: info.ch@tharpa.com

Index

The letter 'g' indicates an entry in the glossary.

Further Reading

If you have enjoyed reading this book and would like to find out more about Buddhist thought and practice, here are some other books by Venerable Geshe Kelsang Gyatso Rinpoche that you might like to read. They are all available from Tharpa Publications.

MODERN BUDDHISM
The path of compassion and wisdom

An inspiring handbook of daily practice that is perfectly suited for those seeking solutions within Buddhism to problems of everyday life, as well as for encouraging practitioners of all faiths to deepen their understanding and practice of the spiritual path. For a free eBook or PDF please visit www.emodernbuddhism.com.

GREAT TREASURY OF MERIT
The practice of relying upon a Spiritual Guide

A comprehensive explanation of *Offering to the Spiritual Guide*, one of the most profound meditation practices of Mahayana Buddhism. This book contains a great wealth of spiritual guidance and an indispensable resource for those wishing to integrate all their spiritual practices into the swift Tantric path to full enlightenment. Also available as an eBook.

THE ORAL INSTRUCTIONS OF MAHAMUDRA
The very essence of Buddha's teachings of Sutra and Tantra

This precious book reveals the uncommon practice of Tantric Mahamudra of the Ganden Oral Lineage, which the author received directly from his Spiritual Guide. It explains clearly and concisely the entire spiritual path from the initial preliminary practices to the final completion stages of Highest Yoga Tantra that enable us to attain full enlightenment in this life. Also available as an eBook.